Scripted Vocational Role Plays

Gary Sigler, Ed.D. and
Darla Kay Fitzpatrick, M.Ed.

IEP
RESOURCES

IEP RESOURCES

P.O. Box 930160
Verona, WI 53593-0160

www.iepresources.com

Phone: 1-800-327-4269

Fax: 1.800.942.3865

© 2000–2006 IEP Resources. All rights reserved.
Reproducible resources within this manual may be photocopied for personal use.

ISBN: 1-57861-107-5

Table of Contents

About the Authors

Gary Sigler, Ed.D.

Gary Sigler has been involved in special education at all grade levels for the past 30 years. His experience includes teaching in elementary schools and at residential secondary facilities, and in teacher preparation at university undergraduate and graduate levels. He currently writes, consults, and is involved in educational programs with the Washington State Department of Corrections.

Darla Kay Fitzpatrick, M.Ed., M.S.

Darla Kay Fitzpatrick has been a special education teacher since 1989. Her experience also includes teaching in regular education classrooms, and working as an educational consultant, writer, and as an instructor for the Heritage Institute in Seattle, Washington. She currently teaches in a self-contained special education classroom for behavior disordered students at Cheney Middle School, in Cheney, WA.

Introduction

Preparing For the World of Work

The ten chapters of role plays in this volume represent many of the essential work-related skills that students need for successful transition to the adult working world. The United States Department of Labor estimates that the majority of workers lose their jobs due to poor work-related skills — not because of their inability to do the job. Consequently, effective vocational training must include adequate work-related skills training to enable students to make a successful transition to the world of work. The role plays in this volume are a valuable assistance for the training of students in work-related skills.

Role Plays Benefit Students

We chose the role play method of teaching for a number of reasons. We believe that for learning to be optimized, it needs to be relevant, interesting, and, ideally, taught in an environment as close as possible to the actual settings where the activities will ultimately take place. For students, relevance is the foundation of meaning. The role plays, then, provide a means of delivering instruction in which students can take an active role in the learning experience. When students become actively involved in relevant learning experiences the skills are more easily transferred, attending to task is increased, and mastering the objectives occurs more quickly. When role plays are supplemented by visiting employers or employment agency personnel, or with field trips to work sites (as suggested in the enrichment sections), students will view first-hand the application of the information they are being taught.

Benefits For Teachers

The essential materials for conducting the role plays have been carefully prepared by the authors. The materials were field tested, evaluated, and revised for effective use in classrooms. As a result, they are ready-to-use in the classroom without further modification or planning. Teachers may enhance the role plays by using the enrichment section of the teacher's guide for each role play. Additionally, the materials are especially effective when they are integrated with related materials, field trips, and appearances by guest speakers. Teachers are encouraged to supplement the materials with creative ideas of their own and learning experiences that fit the particular needs and location of a student. Some topics may be particularly meaningful for students, and these topics provide yet another level of invaluable, real-life preparation; they bring relevance and value to the vocational training experience.

Introduction

Accommodations

Students with reading difficulties may need special consideration to fully participate in the role plays. One suggestion would be to rehearse the scripts during the usual reading instruction time. Rehearsals of the script could be accomplished by arranging students into small groups which contain strong and weak readers to preview the reading "in group" prior to the actual role play. Another technique would be to pair students with good reading skills with students with less developed skills so that the "team" reads the role play. All of these modifications would allow students with poor reading skills to fully participate in the role plays. An additional benefit of rehearsals in advance of conducting the role play is extra practice on the topic; more practice should further enhance the learning and retention of the objectives.

In some instances, a few students may be initially shy about participating in the role plays. Our field tests revealed that by initially using volunteers to play the roles, the other students soon lost their inhibitions and participated fully.

Easy to Use

Planning of the lesson is complete. The instructional objective, purpose and procedures are clearly stated for each role play and may be used directly on the IEP or lesson plans. The scripts are written, worksheet masters are prepared and introductory and post-discussion topics are suggested. They are ready to be used without additional planning or materials. The role plays can either be xeroxed or printed from the included CD-ROM.

The role plays are planned in such a manner that they can be conducted within the limits of one class period. However, teachers can extend or contract the time depending on specific requirements and desires. Likewise, supplemental materials may be used, but are not required. Our intent is to provide you with material that is easy to use, has value for the vocational training of students, and is enjoyable for everyone.

Gary Sigler, Ed.D.
Darla Kay Fitzpatrick, M.S.

Chapter One

ADA

Teacher's Guide

The ADA is What?

Purpose:

To acquaint the students with the basic points of the Americans with Disabilities Act (ADA).

Objectives:

The students will:

1. State what ADA stands for.
2. Provide three examples of accommodations.
3. Explain why accommodations are needed.

Procedures:

1. Ask the students why _____ wears glasses. How do they help her/him? What would happen if the person were not allowed to wear glasses? What would they be unable to do? Drive? Work? Read? Is it a good idea for the person to wear glasses?
2. Select three students to participate in the role play.
3. Conduct the role play.
4. Review, with the class, the essential points of the role play.
5. Complete the worksheet.

Discussion suggestions:

1. Try to list all of the accommodations that we may see in a day (i.e., sidewalk cuts, ramps, wide stalls in restrooms, wide doors, automatic doors, audio devices on street lights, braces on legs/arms., wheelchairs, canes and crutches, etc.)

Enrichment:

Every college and university has a person that coordinates services to people with disabilities. Ask them to visit your class and describe some of the accommodations they provide.

Worksheet:

The ADA is what?

Worksheet

The ADA is What?

Place a check in front of things that may be considered an accommodation for someone.

_____ Wheelchairs	_____ Medicine
_____ Eyeglasses	_____ Picture signs
_____ Leg braces	_____ Wide doors
_____ A cane	_____ Elevators
_____ Ramps into buildings	_____ Raised letter signs
_____ Curb cuts at corners	_____ Large print books
_____ Hearing aids	_____ Extra time on tests

Role Play

The ADA is What?
Scene:
A student pacing back and forth talking to himself.

Todd:

I didn't get hired because I can't see very well, but I can do the job they want. They wouldn't give me a chance to show them what I can do. If only I could get a chance.

Scene:
Enters Dee, a friend of Todd's.

Dee:

Todd, I didn't hear what you said.

Todd:

Oh, I was just talking to myself about the job I didn't get.

Dee:

Why didn't you get the job?

Todd:

I don't see very well, as you know, and they would not give me a chance.

Dee:

What kind of a job was it, Todd?

Todd:

Software designer. I've done several pieces and they liked them.

Dee:

Then why didn't they hire you?

Role Play

Todd:

They felt that I may not be able to do the work in their offices and complete all of the other tasks of the office as well.

Scene:
Roman enters the conversation that he has been listening to.

Roman:

Wow, Todd, that's really too bad.

Dee:

Do you need anything special to be able to do the work?

Todd:

Yes. I need a large monitor for the computer and a scanner so I can put memos and stuff on the computer and enlarge it so I can read it.

Roman:

Did you tell them you needed that stuff?

Todd:

No, I never did.

Dee:

Maybe they're not aware of how that stuff would allow you to do the work as well as anyone.

Roman:

Right, Todd. You know John. He had to ask his boss to change part of his job so that he would be able to do it.

Role Play

Todd:

   And they did it?

Dee:

   You bet! He's a good worker and they wanted to keep him.

Roman:

   They accommodated for him. It's the law. They have to.

Todd:

   What are accommodations and what law?

Roman:

   The law is the Americans with Disabilities Act. Accommodations are changes to the work place, schools, or transportation and communication systems that allow individuals with special needs to work and have access to places.

Dee:

   Can you say all of that again?

Roman:

   It's simple. People that have special needs to work, travel, learn, or communicate are given accommodations that can allow them to compete with people who have no special needs.

Todd:

   So, if I had told them the equipment I use to be able to work the computers they would have allowed me to have it?

Role Play

Dee:

It worked for John. Sara doesn't read very well so they changed her job so that other people do most of the reading and she does the stock work.

Todd:

I guess that is why there are ramps, instead of stairs, into buildings.

Roman:

Exactly, they're required by the ADA.

Dee:

So people in wheel chairs can get into buildings using ramps.

Todd:

I never thought about it, but I've seen telephones with switches that change how loud they are. That could be part of the ADA.

Roman:

You're right. Both of those things are required by the ADA.

Todd:

And they are called accommodations?

Roman:

That's right!

Todd:

I'll call the company and tell them what I need before they hire someone.

Teacher's Guide

ADA and Higher Education

Purpose:

To acquaint students with the coordinator of services for persons with disabilities at higher education facilities. To present students with some of the kinds of accommodations that can be made for otherwise qualified students.

Objectives:

The students will:

1. Define "Otherwise Qualified."
2. Identify the person to contact at institutions of higher education.
3. Identify three accommodations that would be possible.

Procedure:

1. Discuss with the students the notion of "equal treatment." What does that mean? Is it that all people are treated the same, or that all people are held to the same standards of performance and criteria (note: the latter is correct)?
2. Select three students to participate in the role play.
3. Conduct the role play.
4. Review with the class the essential points of the role play.
5. Complete the worksheet.

Discussion suggestion:

1. Provide each student the opportunity to identify any accommodations for which they may be eligible. Students that are willing can share their thoughts with their classmates.

Worksheet:

ADA and Higher Education

Worksheet

ADA and Higher Education

Write the answer in the blank for each statement.

A person at each post-secondary school that assists students with disabilities is usually called

_____.

A change in the general way of doing things for a student with a disability is called an

_____.

Name a change that could be made to the way tests are given.

_____.

When a person is able to get accommodations they are said to be

_____.

The name of the law that covers all of the above ideas is

_____.

Answers:
Americans with Disabilities Act
Accommodation
More time
Otherwise qualified
Coordinator

Role Play

ADA and Higher Education
Scene:
Two seniors from the local high school talking in a cafe.

Dave:

Hey, Rick, did you hear I'll be able to take the entry exams to go to the state university without having to worry about time limits?

Rick:

Wow. That's cool, John. I imagine you're feeling pretty good.

Dave:

You bet. Plus, I think you could get into the vocational aircraft mechanics program you wanted.

Rick:

How would I do that? I don't meet their qualifications.

Dave:

You can do just what I did. Use the Americans with Disabilities Act (ADA).

Rick:

How would I use it?

Dave:

Listen, if you don't meet the qualifications as a result of disability and you are otherwise qualified then you are covered by the law.

Rick:

Well, I don't meet the qualifications and it is a result of disability, but what is otherwise qualified?

Role Play

Dave:

The way I understand it is if you can do the work, in spite of your disability, then you are otherwise qualified.

Rick:

Well, I can fix anything. And I would love to work on airplanes.

Scene:

Enters Dea, an older friend of Rick and Dave.

Dea:

Hi, Rick. Hi, Dave. How are you guys?

Dave:

Great, Dea. How's it going at the university?

Dea:

Very well. It was difficult at first, but then I learned about a law that helped me.

Rick:

It must have been the ADA.

Dave:

We were just talking about it. How did it help you, Dea?

Dea:

There's a coordinator of services to students with disabilities and she was a great help in letting me know what I could ask for.

Rick:

Do all post-secondary schools have a coordinator?

Role Play

Dea:

Yes. All of them do. You need to contact them before you arrive at the school.

Dave:

What kinds of things does the coordinator help with?

Dea:

All aspects of your education that are impacted by your disability. She arranges accommodations based on what you need.

Rick:

What kinds of things?

Dave:

Like me getting more time on the entrance exam?

Dea:

That's right. Some students get to take exams in private with more time, or with someone to write their answers. Or, they may get to do some other type of test instead of with pencil and paper.

Rick:

Like what kind of test?

Dea:

Well, in your case of aircraft mechanic, they may ask you to do something on a plane instead of telling about it on a test.

Dave:

What else?

Role Play

Dea:

I was in one class that had to change classrooms because a student who used a wheelchair couldn't get to the second floor.

Rick:

I'd do better if I could tape record classes.

Dea:

If your need is part of a disability, then it's possible to arrange that and the coordinator will help you.

Dave:

Sounds like there are a lot of things other than just more time on tests.

Dea:

Yes. Many things you need, because of disability,
or if you are otherwise qualified.

Rick:

Wow, maybe I will be able to go the mechanics school after all. I'll call and ask for the coordinator of services to individuals with disabilities.

Teacher's Guide

ADA and Employment

Purpose:

For students to be aware of the role of the ADA for employment and what it means for workers with disabilities. Students will know what comprises a "good job."

Objectives:

The students will:

1. State two components of a "good job."
2. Cite two examples of accommodations in the work place.
3. State whose responsibility it is to tell employers of their needs.
4. Define what the term "reasonable" means in the ADA.
5. State the limits for employers covered by the ADA.

Procedures:

1. Divide students into small groups and assign to each group a job (i.e., carpenter, retail clerk, janitor, mechanic, bus driver). Then, assign to each group a disability (i.e., reading disability, mobility, hearing, vision, motor skill). Then ask the students to try and figure out how a person with that disability could do the job that has been assigned their group.
2. Select three students to conduct the role play.
3. Conduct the role play.
4. Review the essential points of the role play with the students.
5. Complete the worksheet, ADA and Employment.

Discussion suggestions:

1. Are eye glasses and hearing aides accommodations for workers?
2. Is it fair to employers to ask them to make accommodations?

Enrichment:

Contact your local state vocational rehabilitation office and ask for a counselor to visit the class and describe some of the accommodations they have used to assist workers.

Worksheet:

ADA and Employment

Worksheet

ADA and Employment

Complete the following.

1. There are three parts to having a good job. They are:

_____

_____

_____

2. State two examples of worker accommodations.

_____

_____

3. Who needs to tell the employer about a worker's needs for accommodations?

_____

4. When the term "reasonable accommodation" is used it means that the accommodation may not _____ too much and must not interfere with the _____ of the company.

5. Some companies are not required to follow the ADA. They are those with less than _____ employees.

Words to use in the blanks:

employee	living wage	full time
ramps into buildings	benefits	low tables
cost	other workers	15

Role Play

ADA and Employment
Scene:
Three friends discussing their opportunities for a good job.

Rudy:
I think I have a really good job.

Jodi:
You mean a job that is full-time, pays a living wage, and has benefits?

Rudy:
Right, a GOOD job.

Beth:
How will you be able to do that with a disability that keeps you from doing some things?

Jodi:
Yes, Rudy, how will you be able to overcome that?

Rudy:
Well, you've heard of the Americans with Disabilities Act, haven't you?

Beth:
Sure, will you be able to use some of those rules to assist you?

Rudy:
That's right! Just like at school, there are also rules for "otherwise qualified" workers.

Role Play

Jodi:

So that means that you can have accommodations and be assisted to work more effectively?

Beth:

Like Dave having more time for tests in school?

Rudy:

That's right. I have learned the skills to be an inventory clerk.
Now all I need is the opportunity to do the work.

Jodi:

Well, you can't carry much, and you can't climb a ladder.

Rudy:

That's true. But those things are a pretty small part of the job. I could share or trade some parts of the job with other workers so that if we worked together we could get the job done.

Beth:

And the boss will be willing to do all of that?

Jodi:

I think the law requires that they go along with that.

Rudy:

Most employers are willing to make accommodations. And the law requires that any employer with more than 15 employees has to make "reasonable accommodations."

Role Play

Beth:

Uh-oh, another one of those terms!

Jodi:

What does reasonable accommodations mean?

Rudy:

It means that if a worker is otherwise qualified and needs some changes to the job or the work place then they have a right to get those changes.

Beth:

But what if it costs a lot or interferes with other workers?

Rudy:

Those are both things that need to be considered. If costs are excessive then the employer may be excused.

Jodi:

I'll bet if it interferes with the other workers they don't have to do it, either.

Rudy:

That's right. The workers must be able to continue working.

Beth:

I remember when Sue needed someone at work to do the filing in the top drawer because from her wheelchair she couldn't reach it.

Jodi:

Yes, what they did was have the other workers do that part of the job while Sue answered the telephones for the others.

Role Play

Rudy:

That's a good example of using the ADA to accommodate workers.

Beth:

And it didn't cost the employer anything.

Jodi:

Right! But, what if employers won't make accommodations?

Rudy:

Most of the time they will. But it's up to you to let them know what it is that you need.

Beth:

When would be the best time to do that?

Jodi:

Yeah, it seems like if you asked for a lot of things to begin with you probably wouldn't get the job.

Rudy:

In my case, I interviewed for the job and they asked how I could do some of the parts of it. Then I told them what I needed to do the work.

Beth:

They must have agreed. You got the job.

Jodi:

I think you're right, Rudy. You have a very good job.

Teacher's Guide

Otherwise Qualified

Purpose:
To teach the students the meaning of the terms, "otherwise qualified", "qualified individual", and "reasonable accommodation."

Objectives:
The students will:

1. Define the terms —
   - otherwise qualified
   - qualified individual
   - reasonable accommodation
2. State two limits to reasonable accommodations.

Procedures:

1. Ask the students if they like to help people? Get them to state some ways they help people. Ask them if helping in the workplace is O.K.?
2. Select three students to participate in the role play.
3. Conduct the role play.
4. Review the essential points of the role play.
5. Complete the worksheet.

Discussion suggestion:
Provide examples of disability for the students and ask them to provide examples of accommodations for some common jobs in the community.

Worksheet:
Otherwise Qualified

Worksheet

Otherwise Qualified

Fill in the blanks using the words provided.

1. Reasonable accommodations are changes to the _____ and/or _____ .

2. An otherwise qualified individual is a person that with reasonable accommodations can perform the _____ of the job.

3. Another word for otherwise qualified is _____ .

4. A limit to reasonable accommodations is a very high _____ .

5. Small companies are required to spend _____ than large companies for reasonable accommodations.

6. Companies with less than _____ employees are not required to provide reasonable accommodations

7. Reasonable accommodations must be _____ .

Words to use:

safe	less
qualified individual	job
essential functions	workplace
cost	15

Role Play

Otherwise Qualified
Scene:

Two students viewing the job announcement board at the state employment office.

Marge:

I see a lot of jobs that I could do, but I would need to convince the employer first.

Jill:

Yes, I know. I keep hearing about the ADA and the idea of 'otherwise qualified' but I'm not sure what it means.

Marge:

I have the same problem. I would like to talk with the employers about my ability and use the idea of 'otherwise qualified' but I just don't have the confidence I need.

Jill:

Maybe we should ask the employment counselor when we go in to see him.

Scene:
Jill and Marge are called into the counselor's office.

Mr. Gage:

Well ladies, how are you today?

Marge:

Well, Mr. Gage, we were just talking and find that neither of us are clear on what otherwise qualified means.

Role Play

Jill:

And, what does it mean to us?

Mr. Gage:

I think you know about the ADA. In the ADA an 'otherwise qualified' individual is often called 'qualified individual.'

Marge:

Does that matter to us?

Mr. Gage:

No, you can use either term.

Jill:

So what does it mean?

Mr. Gage:

A qualified individual with a disability is an individual who with reasonable accommodation can perform the essential functions of the job.

Marge:

Now, what does 'reasonable accommodation' mean?

Jill:

It has something to do with cost, right?

Mr. Gage:

Good, Jill. A reasonable accommodation is a change to the job or work place that will allow a person with a disability to perform the job.

Role Play

Marge:

A change to the job or work place? Like what?

Mr. Gage:

Well, your classmate, Sean, could not bend over for long periods of time so we arranged with his employer to raise the work table.

Jill:

That was simple.

Mr. Gage:

Yes, it was. It also helped several other employers that could work standing up instead of bending over all day.

Marge:

What was the thing about cost?

Jill:

If it cost too much they don't need to do it, right?

Mr. Gage:

Yes, but it is not that simple. A very large company could afford to spend more than a small one. A company with less than 15 employees is not required to do it at all.

Marge:

So if I work for a large company a reasonable accommodation could cost a lot more than in a small company.

Role Play

Mr. Gage:

Also, if the accommodations create a safety problem or interfere with the usual work of the company then they will not need to do it, either.

Jill:

So, I can ask for accommodations but they may not get done?

Marge:

If they are very expensive or create a disruption or a safety hazard they won't be done.

Mr. Gage:

I think you get the idea. Most employers are willing to make accommodations if it means they will get or keep a good worker.

Jill:

A woman where my mother worked uses a very big magnifying glass. Is that an accommodation?

Marge:

Sounds like it.

Mr. Gage:

Yes, it is. Some accommodations are complicated and some, like a magnifying glass, are very simple.

Jill:

I feel better now. I think I understand. Thank you, Mr. Gage.

Teacher's Guide

Asking for Accommodations

Purpose:

To assist students in deciding when to advise employers or potential employers about disabilities and the need for accommodations.

Objectives:

The students will:

1. Cite what employers are not allowed to ask applicants.
2. State the rules for when they need to tell the employer about disabilities.

Procedures:

1. With the students in small groups ask each group to list three reasons to tell employers about their disability when applying for a job, and three reasons to wait until they are hired. Provide time for the groups to compare their answers.
2. Select three students to participate in the role play.
3. Conduct the role play.
4. Review with the class the essential points.
5. Complete the worksheet

Discussion suggestions:

1. Why would it be good to tell employers about disabilities when applying?
2. How does the type of disability affect the when It's best to tell the employer?

Worksheet:

Asking for Accommodations

Worksheet

Asking for Accommodations

In front of the following statements place one of the following letters:
A – for telling the employer on the application, I – for telling the employer during the interview,
H – for telling the employer after being hired

_____ A person uses a wheelchair.

_____ An applicant has a mild hearing disability.

_____ The person has severe seizure disorders.

_____ The applicant has very limited vision.

_____ The person has difficulty writing.

_____ The applicant has poor reading skills.

_____ The person has a medical condition for which they take medicine.

_____ The applicant stutters.

Role Play

Asking for Accommodations
Scene:
Two students and their transition teacher having a discussion.

Pat:

I think I understand what accommodations are but I am unsure of when to ask for them.

Ms. Jones:

What is it that puzzles you about that, Pat?

Pat:

Well, if I tell the company when I apply I may not get an interview.

Jeff:

And, if you don't tell them and you get the job you may lose it when you tell them.

Pat:

So when do we say what?

Ms. Jones:

That depends on you and the type of disability.

Jeff:

What part depends on me?

Ms. Jones:

The labor laws are written so that the employers may not ask about age, religion, marriage, disability and other protected areas for discrimination.

Role Play

Pat:

So, if you use a wheelchair they don't need to ask.

Jeff:

But, if you have a medical condition they would need to ask or they would not know.

Ms. Jones:

So the issue is if you should tell before the interview or when you begin work?

Pat:

In my case I don't need much, just a place where I can rest for a few minutes if I feel a seizure coming on.

Ms. Jones:

So you could tell them on the application, at the interview, or wait until you are on the job.

Jeff:

I will need to tell them before the interview because we will need to have a quiet place to interview due to my hearing.

Pat:

Maybe I should have the medical records of my seizure disorder, and an explanation of how often it occurs and how long it lasts.

Ms. Jones:

I'm certain that that would be appreciated.

Role Play

Jeff:

Perhaps, I need a written statement of the accommodations I will need, which aren't much.

Pat:

So what we need to do is provide the company with information about the disability — what we need to help us be good workers.

Jeff:

And when we tell them depends on the nature of our disability, the types of accommodations needed, and our own confidence.

Ms. Jones:

That sounds correct to me.

Pat:

So there are no requirements?

Ms. Jones:

No, none. If the company will need to build a ramp, move a work station, or put in special equipment, then you will need to tell them as soon as possible so they will have time.

Jeff:

In my case, I just need some quiet area to work. Fortunately, the company I am looking at already is very quiet.

Pat:

So, Jeff, you may need to say nothing at all.

Role Play

Ms. Jones:

But Pat, you will need to tell them so that if you have a seizure they will know exactly what is happening.

Jeff:

Right! I know a person that had a seizure and they thought he was on drugs. They were going to fire him.

Pat:

So what I need to decide is when I want to tell them.

Ms. Jones:

Yes, Pat. If they provide a tour of the offices for you you might be able to identify places that will meet your needs.

Jeff:

Then, Pat, you would not need to tell them at all.

Ms. Jones:

No, that wouldn't be a good idea. They need to know so they're aware of the disability and can help if it is needed.

Pat:

Right, I've nothing to hide.

Jeff:

I feel much better about when to tell.

Pat:

Me, too. Thank you, Ms. Jones.

Chapter
Two

Career
Considerations

Teacher's Guide

What to Look for in Your Career

Purpose:

To acquaint students with some of the criteria that should be considered for selecting a career.

Objectives:

The students will:

1. Identify the criteria they desire for a career.
2. Define career, as opposed to job.

Procedures:

1. Ask the students to differentiate between a career and a job. As the students are brainstorming this difference, write some of the key points on the board for discussion later.
2. Select the students to play the roles.
3. Conduct the role play.
4. Follow the discussion suggestions.
5. Complete the worksheet.

Discussion suggestions:

1. What are the advantages of selecting a career according to the criteria presented in the role play?
2. How would your life be different if you just accepted any job you could get?

Enrichment:

Ask the career counselor from your school, a local college, the state employment office, or state vocational rehabilitation office to visit your class and discuss these issue with the students.

Worksheet:

Complete the worksheet.

Worksheet

What to Look for in Your Career

Circle the items that are important for you in your career.

location   training

promotions   pay

travel   job security

benefits   full-time

What else would you like from your career?

_____

_____

Role Play

What to Look for in Your Career
Scene:
Two friends walking across the campus.

Sean:

This search for a career is hard.

Pat:

You know it is.

Sean:

There is so much to consider that I get lost.

Pat:

Yeah, but I have learned a lot and I remember that I want a good job.

Sean:

Yes, I remember the conversation that Pete and Sue had about a "good" job and it sure made sense.

Pat:

You know it did. To have a livable wage, benefits, and permanent year around work seems very important.

Sean:

But, when we look at careers there seems to be so much more to consider.

Pat:

Right. Like training. Did you know that some companies will train their employees in the career field that they have chosen?

Role Play

Sean:

Yes, I've heard that. And, you get paid at the same time.

Pat:

So the idea is to choose a career that has a lot of advancement opportunities for you. Then, look for a company that trains for advancement.

Sean:

I'd like that. To get paid to learn.

Pat:

If you go into a career that has advancement opportunities you could get promoted and make more money.

Sean:

Money! I love money. So the right career, matched with a company that trains you, and then a chance for promotion. What could be better?

Pat:

I want that. And a career in an area that's a growth area. Then, I won't be out of work because that career isn't needed anymore.

Sean:

Yeah, people in the horse buggy business lost careers because cars took the place of buggies.

Pat:

Yeah. It's just not job security, but there's career security, too.

Sean:

That's part of the reason we train for career clusters not just specific jobs.

Role Play

Pat:

Right. Security is having a job and a company in a career field that will continue for a long while.

Sean:

Of course we can always retrain for another career.

Pat:

And go through all of this again? I can and I will, if I need too, but I don't really want to do it.

Sean:

Me neither. But like you, I can do it. And I bet that at sometime we'll have to do it.

Pat:

And then there's the issue of where you want to live.

Sean:

See, I was interested in marine biology. Studying sea animals. But then I figured I would need to move away from here and my family and I don't want to do that.

Pat:

So you needed to make a new choice?

Sean:

Yes, but now I will stay here where all of my friends and family live.

Pat:

I've thought about a career in the military. That will require moving, but I don't mind. In fact, I look forward to it.

Role Play

Sean:

So that part of a military career would suit you fine.

Pat:

There sure are a lot of things to think about .

Sean:

But if we get it right this time we should be able to have good work and pay for the foreseeable future.

Pat:

I like that idea.

Teacher's Guide

Careers, NOT Jobs

Purpose:
To acquaint the students with the difference between careers and jobs.

Objectives:
The students will:
1. State the difference between career clusters and a job.
2. Recognize that occupational field and career clusters are synonymous.
3. Relate two advantages of careers over jobs.

Procedures:
1. Engage the students in a discussion about the kind of work they look forward to doing. List some of the preferences on the board.
2. Select students to complete the role play.
3. Conduct the role play.
4. Follow the discussion suggestions
5. Complete the worksheet.

Discussion suggestions:
1. Discuss with the students the ideas you put on the board earlier. Were these ideas career clusters/occupational fields, or were they jobs?
2. Ask the students to identify jobs related to the ones listed on the board that would expand the single jobs into career clusters/occupational fields.

Enrichment:
Ask the students to identify jobs in the community (as they shop, play, etc.). Ask them to group jobs into occupational fields or career clusters. Have the students report their findings within a few days.

Worksheet:
Careers, NOT Jobs.

Worksheet

Careers, NOT Jobs

1. A career cluster has many jobs within the career. A job is a specific job within a career cluster. Circle all of the jobs in the list below.

grocery clerk   retail clerk

machine operator   drill press operator

shoe salesperson   retail salesperson

bus driver   commercial vehicle driver

house framer   carpenter

2. Check the statements that are advantages of having training for a career cluster.

_____ You are qualified for many jobs.

_____ If you lose a particular job you can apply for many specific jobs depending on what is available.

_____ If you have training in a career cluster and you move to a new area, your chances of getting a job are better than if you just trained for a job.

_____ Your employer can use you in more ways.

_____ Training for a new job, in the same career cluster, is easy.

_____ If you want to change your job it will be easier for you.

Role Play

Careers, NOT Jobs

Scene 1:
Two friends sitting on a park bench.

Linda:
Well, Sandy, I just don't have a clue of what to work toward.

Sandy:
It can be tough to decide.

Linda:
Ms. Taylor suggested that I consider an occupational field rather than a particular job.

Sandy:
What does that mean?

Linda:
She said that an occupational field would be a collection of specific jobs that are all very similar.

Sandy:
Like you get paid for all of them?

Linda:
No, I think it was more than that. But it was difficult because she didn't have much time to explain.

Role Play

Sandy:

I know I can't explain. I've never heard of it before.

Scene 2:

Pete is walking along and joins in with the girls.

Pete:

Hi, Sandy. Hi, Linda. What's up?

Linda:

We were trying to decide what Ms. Taylor meant when she was explaining some career stuff to me.

Sandy:

You had the career education class didn't you, Pete?

Pete:

Yes, last quarter, it was great!

Linda:

Then maybe you can explain what she meant by occupational field. Then she used another term — career cluster. And I got confused.

Pete:

Well, I think they mean the same thing.

Sandy:

Help us a little, Pete. What do they mean?

Role Play

Pete:

Well the idea is to train into a field or a cluster of jobs instead of just one job.

Linda:

Yeah, I remember that! Instead of training for a specific job she said I could train for a group of jobs.

Sandy:

Give me an example.

Pete:

Well, I decided I wanted to be a grocery checkout clerk.

Sandy:

Is that a cluster or a field?

Linda:

Neither one. That's a job, isn't it, Pete?

Pete:

Right. I had decided on a specific job. Ms. Taylor suggested that I train for more than the job.

Sandy:

Like what?

Pete:

Like a cluster of related jobs, a career cluster, or occupational field.

Role Play

Sandy:

I still need examples.

Linda:

Help me out, Pete. If you trained for work as a retail clerk you would be able to work in grocery stores, drug stores, department stores and other similar jobs as a clerk right?

Pete:

You got it. All of those jobs are very similar. By being prepared for all of them I had a better chance of getting a good job.

Sandy:

OK. If, you train for a single job you will have less jobs to apply for and less chance of getting a good job.

Linda:

But, if you train for a cluster of jobs that are similar, you can apply for any of them.

Pete:

Even better, I have a variety of job skills. So if something were to happen to my job I could easily take another type of retail clerk job.

Sandy:

Sounds good. How did it work?

Pete:

I've gotten a good job at Major Grocery. It pays a good wage, I get benefits, and it's full-time permanent work!

Role Play

Linda:

Now I can decide on a specific job and then see where it fits into a cluster. Or, I can decide on a general occupational field and pick the specific job from what is available later.

Teacher's Guide

Career Training Decisions

Purpose:
To provide students insight into the training considerations associated with selecting careers.

Objectives:
The students will:
1. Name four career training methods.
2. Identify three associated training concerns (cost, location, duration).

Procedures:
1. Assign the students to several small groups and assign each group with the task of listing as many career training methods as they can. Compare the lists and announce the group with the longest list.
2. Select students to participate in the role play.
3. Conduct the role play.
4. Follow the discussion suggestions.
5. Complete the worksheet.

Discussion suggestions:
1. Is cheaper better for training?
2. Is shorter better for training?
3. Can you go to any college for any career?

Enrichment:
1. Select several colleges within your region and collect their college catalogs. Have the students compare the catalogs to find programs that some schools have that the others don't offer.
2. Ask the students to use the catalogs to compare the costs of tuition, room and board, and other fees.
3. Have students compare the annual costs of travel to and from each college.

Worksheet:
Career Training Decisions.

Worksheet

Career Training Decisions
Use the list of words and terms to complete the sentences.

college or university   graduate school

trade/vocational school   community colleges

on-the-job training   vocational programs

1. A _____ has programs that most often take about four years to complete.

2. These _____ programs are after the completion of college or university and often train professionals such as doctors.

3. _____ provide academic programs for people that will go to colleges or universities later and a variety of vocational programs.

4. A way to get trained and paid at the same time is to go into _____ programs.

5. Sometimes called work/study these high school _____ get you ready for a job when graduate from high school.

6. A vocational school, often private, that trains people for specific careers is called a _____.

Role Play

Career Training Decisions
Scene:
Two students sitting on a campus bench, chatting.

Kara:

It sure has been interesting learning about careers in the career opportunities class with Mr. Bryce.

Jose:

Yeah. I've learned a lot, and most of it I wouldn't have thought of on my own.

Kara:

What was important for you from the class?

Jose:

Well, I had given some thought to what I wanted to do but I really hadn't given thought to training.

Kara:

I know what you mean. Like where, when, cost, and all of that.

Jose:

I always thought being a lawyer would be interesting until I found out that I would have to go to school for at least seven years after high school.

Kara:

Wow, that long?

Jose:

Yep! Four years of college and then three years of law school. And, to tell you the truth, I don't read as well as I would like.

Role Play

Kara:

I'll bet there is a lot of reading to become a lawyer.

Jose:

I learned that they may need to read and understand 500 pages a week. I guess I could get some help, like I do now, but I wouldn't enjoy the pressure.

Kara:

I can understand that. I've looked into being a bank teller and found that the school for that was six months to a year long. I can do it.

Jose:

That sounds good. Where is the school?

Kara:

Well there is a private vocational school on the east side and there's a program at the community college.

Jose:

So there are both private vocational schools and the community college right here in town?

Kara:

Yeah, isn't that great?

Jose:

Sure is! It should keep the cost down. That's important to me.

Kara:

Cost is important. The community college is cheaper but a bit longer than the private vocational school. But there is no travel and those costs.

Role Play

Jose:

My brother decided to become a carpenter. He was able to enter the trade association on-the-job training program.

Kara:

How does that work?

Jose:

He applied to the trade association and was placed with a contractor during the day making a beginning wage. During the week he goes to two night classes.

Kara:

Cool! Pay and training all in one. What does he do at the night classes?

Jose:

He learns about building techniques, measuring, regulations, inspections, all that stuff.

Kara:

Isn't the program for three years?

Jose:

Yes, but he gets a raise each year and has benefits, too.

Kara:

Melinda took the nurse's aide program through the high school and she will be trained and ready to work when she graduates.

Jose:

I've noticed that she was never around at lunch and afterward. Isn't that the program where students attend here in the mornings then do something else in the afternoons?

Role Play

Kara:

Yes. She goes to regular classes then to nurse's aide training and gets experience in the afternoon.

Jose:

She's ahead of us. She'll be trained at the end of high school.

Kara:

There are a lot of choices and options.

Jose:

Sure are! There are community colleges, colleges and universities, after college schools like law school . . . .

Kara:

It's part of the career decision knowing what the training options are and what's required — like at trade schools, trade association on-the-job programs, work study like Melinda, and probably a lot more!

Teacher's Guide

What Can I Do for My Career?

Purpose:
To provide a guide to students for selecting a career.

Objectives:
The students will:
1. Use their aptitudes/skills as part of the career selection process.
2. Identify the training required for considered careers.
3. Determine their interest in the type of work involved with the career.

Procedures:
1. Brainstorm with the students and develop a list of desired careers. Then, ask the students to separate the realistic careers from the fantasy careers. Reality careers are those for which there is accessible training, jobs, interest, and aptitude.
2. Select students to participate in the role play.
3. Conduct the role play.
4. Use the discussion suggestions to review with the students
5. Complete the worksheet, individually or in group.

Discussion suggestions:
1. How would you decide if the training for a desired career is good for you?
2. How important is it that there are jobs, in your community, for the career you select?

Enrichment:
Ask a teacher in your building to come to your class and discuss with the students how they selected teaching as a career (you may want to do some interviewing yourself, prior to teacher selection).

Worksheet:
What Can I Do for My Career?

Worksheet

What Can I Do for My Career?

1. My best subjects in school are (circle yours):

math	writing
reading	English
social studies	history
shop classes	art
business classes	computer
physical education	

2. My favorite two hobbies are:

   _____

   _____

3. Do my best school subjects match my hobbies?   Yes   No

4. Are there careers in which I could use my hobbies and best school subjects?
   If, yes, list one here _____
   If, no, ask your teacher to assist you to find some that will.

Role Play

What Can I Do for My Career?
Scene:
Three students are standing and talking

Pete:
What's the trouble, Sue?

Sue:
I just left the counselor's office and she reminded me that I need
to decide on a career. You know — the kind of work I will do after we graduate.

Jake:
Sounds like a good idea.

Sue:
Sure it is. But, I don't have any career ideas.

Pete:
There must be a lot of choices.

Sue:
So many that I am confused!

Jake:
What are your best classes in school?

Sue:
Shop classes. I love to build things.

Role Play

Pete:

That may be a start. What kind of careers are there where
you could build things?

Sue:

I'm not sure. My Uncle is a baker. He builds bread, pies and things like that.

Jake:

I hadn't thought of baking as building things, but, I guess it is. My cousin, who
graduated two years ago, is taking auto body repair at the community college.
He rebuilds cars.

Sue:

I could do that. I like anything where I use my hands to create or fix things.

Pete:

Why not make a list of of jobs that would allow you to use your hands
and create things.

Sue:

Sure. Then even if I couldn't find one of those jobs, maybe I could find ones that
require similar skills.

Pete:

Exactly! My cousin takes auto painting, body work, and some mechanics, too.
By taking all three he is training in one career field.

Jake:

That's neat. Then, he can work in any of those areas with
just a little extra training.

Role Play

Pete:

That is what he said, too. So make your list. Then, you need to decide what skills you need to do that kind of work.

Sue:

I will need to make sure I can get training for the career, too.

Pete:

Sure. We have two years of high school left where you may get some training. Then there is the community college, vocational school, and sometimes even on-the-job training.

Sue:

You both have helped a lot. Let's see what I need to do. I need to:
• Make a list of jobs that are of interest to me.
• Group the jobs by the skills I have now.
• Decide what training I will need.
• Find out where and how I can get trained.

Jake:

That's right, Sue, you need to train for a specific job within a group of jobs like auto repair trades.

Sue:

I've got it!

Pete:

Good luck, Sue. Oh, be sure that the career you train for is needed in the community, too.

Role Play

Sue:

I'll need to figure out how to do that!

Jake:

The counselor will help you with that.

Teacher's Guide

Getting Ideas for a Career

Purpose:
To provide students with sources of ideas that will assist them in identifying career options.

Objectives:
The student will:

1. Name three sources of ideas and information for careers.
2. Name a source of information on availability of employment in a career field.

Procedures:
1. Assemble the students in small groups and ask them to assist one another to develop a list of sources of information concerning careers. Ask some of the groups to share their lists with the class.
2. Select students to participate in the role play.
3. Conduct the role play.
4. Utilize the discussion suggestions.
5. Complete the worksheet.

Discussion suggestions:
1. What benefit to you are these sources of information?
2. Can you come up with other sources that will assist you?

Enrichment:
Have the students access the Yellow Page government, business, and education sections to identify additional sources of information.

Worksheet:
Getting Ideas for a Career.

Worksheet

Getting Ideas for a Career

Check the three sources of information and ideas that you are most likely to use.

_____ Trade associations and unions

_____ People I know that have careers

_____ State agencies, like the employment office

_____ Recruiters for military service

_____ Local newspapers

_____ National newspapers

_____ Interest inventories

_____ Career classes

List where you will find the trends for various careers:

_____

Role Play

Getting Ideas for a Career
Scene:
A teacher and students are discussing careers in an office.

Brad:
Yeah, I think I understand about jobs and career clusters.

Mr. Great:
Good. There are important differences.

Brad:
Yes, the career cluster, or group of similar jobs, will provide me with more job options. I want that advantage when I finish.

Mr. Great:
What career field have you decided upon.

Brad:
That's the problem. I just don't know what is available.

Joe:
The world of work is yours for the asking.

Brad:
But, what?

Mr. Great:
What does your father do?

Role Play

Brad:

He is an electronic assembler and he says that that is a job that may not be available here for much longer.

Joe:

It's important that the jobs are available.

Mr. Great:

Yes, you will want to select careers that will be here for the foreseeable future. What do your neighbors do?

Brad:

Mr. Sams is an engineer and Ms. Homes is a medical technician.

Mr. Great:

You could talk with them about their careers. Sounds like those occupational fields will be here for a while longer.

Brad:

Sure does.

Mr. Great:

Have you taken the Interest Inventory that we give each spring?

Joe:

That was a big help for me!

Brad:

What is that?

Role Play

Mr. Great:

It's a survey that takes your interests and relates them to specific career fields.

Brad:

So it will make the selections for me?

Mr. Great:

No. It will give you information to help you decide.

Joe:

It's a good way to start.

Mr. Great:

We have you signed up for the career exploration class next quarter. You should get some ideas from there.

Brad:

Good. Johnny said that he was going to the Navy recruiter to get information about being in the Navy. I could do that.

Mr. Great:

Yes. Military recruiters can give you good information. Have you been to the state employment office?

Brad:

No. What would they do?

Mr. Great:

They will have information about jobs that are available, and which jobs areas are increasing and shrinking. Some have classes for career information.

Role Play

Joe:

They do a lot. Don't some trade groups provide information about their trades?

Mr. Great:

Yes, some do. In this area, the construction trade organizations and unions have both information and apprenticeships for training.

Brad:

I'm sure getting ideas of where to look. My mother suggested looking in the newspaper for ideas, too.

Mr. Great:

Yes, the want ads can be helpful to see what jobs are available.

Brad:

Wow. I'll need to talk to people I know, read local papers, take an interest test, see the recruiters, and …

Joe:

You better start soon, you've a lot to do!

Chapter
Three

Looking for
a Job

Teacher's Guide

Labor Market Surveys

Purpose:
To introduce the use of Labor Market Surveys (LMS) for determining the availability of an occupation or job within a community.

Objectives:
The student will:

1. Identify the essential steps in a LMS.
2. Describe the purpose of the LMS.
3. Explain when a LMS would be useful for them.

Procedures:

1. Lead a discussion on how one would find a particular job in the community. After the students have provided a few obvious ways (i.e., reading the paper, applying at companies, etc.) then ask if it would be useful to know if there were actually some of those kinds of jobs in the community, and how many of those jobs were available over the course of a year?
2. Select students to participate in the role play.
3. Conduct the role play.
4. Review with the class the essential points.
5. Complete the worksheet.

Discussion suggestions:

1. What if you were looking for a job that was not available in your community?
2. Would a LMS save or waste time?

Enrichment:
Ask the students to draw a chart showing how they would search for employment illustrating where LMS would fit into their employment-seeking plan.

Worksheet:
Labor Market Surveys

Worksheet

Labor Market Surveys

Number the following statements in the order they are used for doing a Labor Market Survey.

_____ Call each number on your list.

_____ Make a list of likely employers.

_____ Ask the employers if they use the type of job you are interested in.

_____ Ask the employers how many workers they have hired for that job in the past year.

Circle the benefits of using Labor Market Surveys.

Saves time.

You will get a job.

Lets you know if your job skill is needed.

You may learn of current openings.

You are working smart.

Role Play

Labor Market Surveys
Scene:
Three students are sitting at a lunch table, talking.

Darla:

No job, no job, no job!

Gary:

Look smart, act smart, be smart!

Darla:

What do you mean? Are you so smart?

Gary:

I mean there are a lot of jobs, but you need to know how to find them and then just do it.

Rory:

Right, like *you* know.

Gary:

Well, I have a job and neither of you do!

Darla:

You could be smart or just lucky.

Rory:

But, he has a job and we don't.

Role Play

Darla:

O.K., Gary, how did you get a job?

Gary:

Well, at first, I was looking for a job as a short order cook. You know the training I took last year.

Rory:

So you got a short order cook job?

Gary:

No, I got smart. I was reading the want ads, sending resumes, and going to the state employment office.

Darla:

Sounds pretty good. So why didn't you get a job?

Gary:

Because there are only a few short order cooks in this area and there are very few, if any, openings each year.

Rory:

Sounds pretty smart to me. Looking for a job for which there are no openings.

Darla:

That is not too bright. But, you did get a job.

Gary:

Right. When I was not getting anywhere I asked my worker at the state employment office for help.

Role Play

Rory:

What happened?

Gary:

She said to do a labor market survey to see if there were short order cook jobs in the area.

Darla:

What is that?

Gary:

I made a list of community businesses that may use short order cooks, and then I called each one on my list.

Rory:

Sounds easy.

Gary:

It is. I asked if they used short order cooks. If they did, I asked how many had they hired in the past year.

Darla:

And you learned that there were no short order cooks used in the area?

Gary:

No. I learned that there were not as many as I thought and that there had been no openings in the past year.

Rory:

But you got a job.

Role Play

Gary:

Yes! When I called the hospital they did not have a short order job but they did have a prep cook job.

Darla:

But, you are not a prep cook.

Gary:

True, but I have skills that are similar to a prep cook's from my training. So I applied for the job of prep cook.

Rory:

Well at least you have a job, if not the one you really wanted.

Gary:

True. But the hospital provides permanent work, good pay, and benefits.

Darla:

Maybe when they have an opening for short order cook you will be able to move into that job.

Rory:

That would be great, wouldn't it?

Gary:

Yes, they said that they offer job openings to employees of the hospital first, so there is a good chance that I will get the job.

Role Play

Darla:

So to be smart about searching for work I need to _____ of possible employers, call each one and ask if they hire _____, and ask those that do how many they have _____ in the last year.

Gary:

Then you will not look for jobs that don't exist and may find a job opening you would like!

Teacher's Guide

Networking for a Job

Purpose:

To introduce the students to the use of networking as a tool to assist in finding employment.

Objectives:

The students will:

1. Describe the process of "networking."

2. Demonstrate how they would begin networking for their job seeking.

3. Name three individuals that they could use in their network.

Procedures:

1. Introduce the notion of networking to the students by:

    a). Defining the term: Networking is the communication with friends, relatives, and acquaintances for the purpose of finding employment opportunities.

    Note: Networking is simply the communication with others for information concerning jobs. The old adage "it is not what you know but who you know" fits the use of networking. Sometimes a job seeker may have a friend that knows the owner of a company and can thereby get an interview when a direct application will fail.

    b). Use some examples of how and with whom networking could be used. (i.e. parents, aunts, uncles, friends, and by calling, visiting, or writing.)

2. Select students to be the role players.

3. Conduct the role play.

4. Discuss the uses and initiation of networking.

5. Complete the worksheet.

Discussion suggestions:

1. When to use networking?

2. Benefits of networking?

Enrichment:

Have the students draw charts of how their networks would look. Generally, they would place themselves in the middle and then put around the edges the significant individuals with which they would network. They may have lines that would indicate how the network individuals may communicate with one another.

Worksheet:

Networking for a Job

Worksheet

Networking for a Job

1 Write the names of three people you can ask for assistance and information concerning work.

_____

_____

_____

2. Check below the ways you think they may help you.

_____ Refer you to a company that may need new people.

_____ Give you the name of a person that you may talk with.

_____ Tell you about a job opening.

_____ Ask others that they know about the opportunities for you.

3. You could contact the people in your network by:

_____ telephone

_____ in person

_____ mail

Role Play

Networking for a Job
Scene:
Three people are standing by a car.

Archie:
Hi, Jean. What have you been doing?

Jean:
I've been looking for a job.

Archie:
Ugh! That is awfully hard.

Jean:
Yes. It is much harder than I would have guessed it would be.

Archie:
I hear that McKenze took a class on finding jobs and has some good ideas.

Jean:
I should talk with her. Oh, here she comes, now.

Archie:
Hey, McKenze. Jean and I were just talking about you.

McKenze:
Oh yeah? What were you saying?

Role Play

Jean:

We were talking about how to find a job. Archie said that you took a class and got some good ideas.

Mckenze:

Well, yes. It was very useful for me.

Archie:

What did you find the most useful, McKenze?

McKenze:

One of the ways to find a job I should have known, but had never thought of was called networking.

Jean:

What is networking?

Mckenze:

Basically, it's just talking with people you know to get information about jobs and employers.

Archie:

How does that help?

McKenze:

How many people do you two know? Twenty or thirty people each, I'd guess.

Jean:

How does that help me get a job?

Role Play

McKenze:

Some of those people are employed, know employers, or have friends that hire people to work.

Archie:

But, they don't hire anyone themselves.

McKenze:

True. But, they know people that do hire and they can introduce you or get you an interview.

Jean:

So if I were to make a list of people I know that may know of jobs or people who hire workers, then ...

Archie:

Right. You tell them you need a job and ask if they can help you!

McKenze:

You got it. My uncle told my father that he needed a job. My father then called the personnel manager at Ourtown Industries that he knows through church.

Jean:

Then the personnel manager called your uncle?

McKenze:

Not quite. He told my father that there was an opening and that my uncle should call him and say that he had talked with my dad.

Archie:

So it didn't get him a job.

Role Play

Jean:

No, but it got him to the person that could hire him.

McKenze:

Right. It opened the door to the opportunity.

Jean:

It sure would help me. I can't seem to get past the applications.

McKenze:

My uncle got the job and he had never thought of applying at Ourtown.

Archie:

So I could use networking to find_____ and locate companies that may _____.

Jean:

Wow! I can think of five people to call right now.

McKenze:

Good luck!

Teacher's Guide

Who are the Employers in this Area?

Purpose:
To introduce the students to several approaches for locating employers within the community.

Objectives:
The students will:
1. Name five sources of employer information.
2. Describe how/where to access each source of information they name.

Procedures:
1. Select students to play the roles.
2. Write on the board the following terms OR, if you choose to brainstorm during the role play, then wait until then to use the terms:

state employment office   company employment office   yellow pages

newspaper   Chamber of Commerce   library reference desk

city hall   state vocational rehabilitation office   Internet

3. Conduct the role play.
4. Discuss with the class the essential terms that have been listed.
5. Complete the worksheet.

Discussion suggestions:
1. Additional methods of learning of employers.
2. Review definition of a "good job."
3. Ideas of where to turn when all else fails. (i.e. state employment office counselor, successful relative, friends who have good jobs.)

Enrichment:
Invite a counselor from the state employment office to your class to discuss how to find a job and how to use the services of the state office.

Worksheet:
Who are the Employers in This Area?

Worksheet

Who are the Employers in this Area?

1. Name a book that you have at home that is a source of information about employers.
   _____

2. How could you use a computer to learn about potential employers? _____

3. Name an organization that employers belong to that can be found in most all communities.
   _____

4. If you were to use the library you would go to the _____

5. This is a good source of all kinds of news and information, and it's available in every community _____

6. Every large employer has one and they are there just to talk with people about employment.
   _____

7 A state office for the assistance of people to find work. They also provide unemployment benefits. _____

8. A state office for assisting people with work-limiting injuries due to disabilities; it can also help you locate employers. _____

Role Play

Who are the Employers in this Area?
Scene:
Friends talking.

Jake:

I sure would like to find a job.

Lydia:

Where have you looked?

Jake:

Where can you look? There are very few jobs in this town.

Lydia:

So you feel like there is no place for you to work?

Jake:

That's right. And all of the jobs are already filled.

Lydia:

But, it seems like there are a lot of businesses around. Someone must need some kind of help.

Jake:

Sure there are businesses. But before I moved here, I went to school and learned how to be a warehouse worker.

Lydia:

So the problem is that you don't know where to look.

Role Play

Jake:

I guess that's right. I don't know who or where to ask?

NOTE: At this point the role play could be stopped and the class asked to brainstorm the possible ways to find who and where to ask about a warehouse worker job. Upon the conclusion of the brainstorming, the role play could be competed. The role play will NOT exhaust all of the ways to find employers and leads.

Lydia:

My Dad always goes to the State employment office when he needs work. Have you checked there?

Jake:

No. I'm not eligible for unemployment checks because I haven't worked long enough to qualify.

Lydia:

I don't think you have to get unemployment to get help finding a job there. Why don't you check with them? They could help.

Jake:

I guess I should. I walked through the industrial area but didn't see any help wanted signs.

Lydia:

You could stop and ask at the company employment offices. Or, better yet, why not just call the companies and ask?

Jake:

I didn't know you could just call them. It will take a lot of walking to get many names of companies.

Role Play

Lydia:

Why not just look in the Yellow Pages under the kinds of businesses that would use warehouse workers?

Jake:

That's a good idea. I could look under manufacturing, shipping, freight hauling, storage. I wonder what else?

Lydia:

I'm sure that once you start you will find lots in the Yellow Pages.

Jake:

I even check the newspaper once in a while. I should do it every day, I guess.

Lydia:

Once, my brother found a job by calling the Chamber of Commerce. They had a list of businesses in town and he used it to help him contact employers. It worked!

Jake:

That's an idea worth trying! It seems like there should be some kind of information about companies and jobs in this area. Maybe at the library reference desk or city hall or employment office. Once I knew a guy that got some information from the vocational rehabilitation office, even though he didn't actually qualify for their services.

Lydia:

Wow, we really came up with some good ideas! And don't forget the Internet if you have a computer.

Role Play

Jake:
Never would have thought of some of this stuff without your help. But I need to get started. There's a lot to do!

Teacher's Guide

Finding Jobs on the Internet

Purpose:
To familiarize students with availability of job findings on the Internet.

Objectives:
The students will:

1. Identify the Internet as a place to find job openings.
2. Describe how to find job information on the Internet.

Procedures:

1. Discuss with students the use of the Internet: Its role in finding information about a wide range of topics and where computers with on-line capabilities can be found (i.e. libraries, universities, job service centers, etc.).
2. Select students to play the roles.
3. Conduct the role play.
4. Discuss the key terms and concepts:

Internet	Internet address	Access to Internet	Searching the Internet
Web page	Online	Search engine	

5. Complete the worksheet

Discussion suggestions:

1. The range of information available on the Internet.
2. The range of services available on the Internet.
3. How will You use the Internet?

Enrichment:

1. Invite a computer expert to your class to discuss the uses and future on the Internet.
2. Demonstrate the use of the Internet on a school computer.

Worksheet:
Finding Jobs on the Internet.

Worksheet

Finding Jobs on the Internet

1. Circle the ways you could get an Internet address for a company.

   Call the company

   Ask a friend

   Use a search engine

2. Circle the information you might get from the Internet about a job.

   Job description/requirements

   Job openings

   Pay

   Location

   General information about the company

   Benefits

   Hours

3. Circle the advantages of using the Internet in your job search:

   Time saving

   Can look at a lot of companies

   Know a job is available before applying

   Learn a lot about the job

4. Circle the sources of Internet access.

   School

   Libraries

   State Employment offices

Role Play

Finding Jobs on the Internet
Scene:

Seth, Summer and Joel are talking about the difficulty of looking for jobs and finding new job leads.

Summer:

I sure have had a hard time finding job leads.

Seth:

I know what you mean, it is tough.

Summer:

I looked at the State Employment office, the newspaper, and have asked everyone I know. I still can't find a job!

Joel:

It seems that you have looked everywhere but one of the most obvious places.

Seth:

OK wise man, where would you suggest?

Joel:

The same place you spend all that time playing games … on your computer!

Summer:

I've played a lot of games on the computer and have never gotten a job offer.

Joel:

I doubt that you're going to get a job offer by playing games, but you might if you use the computer for finding jobs.

Role Play

Seth:

How do you do that?

Joel:

One way would be to find a company's Internet address.

Summer:

Then what would I do?

Joel:

Log onto the Internet, enter the address, and get the company's web page.

Seth:

That will get me a "good job"?

Joel:

Not quite. The web page will lead you to the job openings that the company may have.

Summer:

So that leaves me almost where I am now. I still haven't applied and don't have an interview.

Seth:

Right, I want a job, not computer practice!

Joel:

Think about it. With the Internet, you know if they have openings that you could apply for and if they do you may be able to apply online.

Role Play

Summer:
You can apply online?

Joel:
Sometimes!

Seth:
Let's see. If I can find the job by using the company's online address, then I may be able to apply online.

Joel:
For most companies you can do all of that, but for some you will need to call or write them.

Summer:
What if I don't know the company's Internet address?

Joel:
You could call the company and ask for it.

Seth:
Or, you could access a search engine and find all references to the company.

Summer:
Good idea, Joel. Do all companies have web pages?

Joel:
No, not all companies. Most of the major companies have them.

Role Play

Seth:

So, in an hour or two I could search a lot of companies and see if they had jobs that I could qualify for.

Summer:

And, I could apply only at companies that I know have current openings.

Joel:

That's right! Not only can you apply for a lot of jobs, but you know in advance that there are openings.

Seth:

What else can I learn online?

Joel:

Most of the web pages include information about the company, pay, benefits, location of jobs and more.

Summer:

I could search for a job and never leave the computer.

Seth:

Except for an interview — and when you get the job.

Joel:

Good luck on your job searches. Let me know how you do.

Summer and Joel:

Thanks, Joel.

Sample Internet Addresses

America's Job Bank	www.ajb.dni.us/
Boeing	www.boeing.com
Club Fed	www.clubfed.com
Employment and Training Administration	www.doleta.gov
Help Wanted USA	www.crm21.com
Hewlett-Packard	www.hp.com
International Career Connection	www.icc.com
Itron	www.itron.com
Itronix	www.itronix.com
Kaiser Aluminum	www.kaiseral.com
Navy Terminal Access Program	www.ncts.navy.mil
The Army Tour	www.goarmy.com
U. S. Bank	www.usbank.com
U. S. Department of Labor	www.dol.gov
U. S. West	www.uswest.com
Wismer Martin	www.wismer.com

Teacher's Guide

What Is A Good Job

Purpose:
To acquaint the students with the desirability for employment to be permanent, pay a living wage, and to provide benefits. A GOOD JOB IS ONE THAT IS PERMANENT, PAYS A LIVING WAGE, AND HAS BENEFITS.

Objectives:
The students will:

1. Cite the benefits of permanent employment.
2. Be able to discuss the benefit of a livable wage.
3. Recognize the advantages of having benefits.

Procedures:

1. Introduce the ideas of permanent, livable wage, and benefits.
2. Select two students to play the roles.
3. Perform the role play.
4. Assist the student in the role of Pete, with the blanks if needed, or allow the class to assist.
5. Discuss some of the main aspects of the role play (permanent, benefits, livable wage).

Discussion suggestions:

1. The value of permanent employment over short-term high/higher pay jobs.
2. The need for employer-provided benefits.
3. The types of benefits:

   retirement plans   health insurance   dental insurance   profit sharing

   disability insurance   life insurance   vacation time   paid leaves

4. Opportunities for advancement and/or additional training.

Enrichment:
Ask the students to observe jobs in the community during their daily/weekly activities. Make a list of the jobs and have discussions with the class on which of the jobs are "good jobs."

Worksheet:
What is a Good Job?

Worksheet

What is a Good Job

What kinds of things make a job a Good Job? Place a check in front of the statement that best describes a Good Job.

_____ High paying, temporary, fun work

_____ Low paying permanent work with benefits

_____ A job that pays a living wage and is easy to do

_____ Good pay, benefits from the employer, and permanent work

_____ A high paying job, without benefits, but fun

_____ A job has employer provided benefits, is fun, and easy

_____ A livable wage with benefits from the employer

Role Play

What Is A Good Job?
Scene:
Two students discussing the merits of jobs.

Pete:

Hi, Sue. Did you hear I got a cool job?

Sue:

No, Pete. That's great.

Pete:

Yeah, and I can make a lot of money.

Sue:

Is the work permanent and year around?

Pete:

Not exactly.

Sue:

What does not exactly mean?

Pete:

It's a seasonal job, but I'll make a lot of money per hour.

Sue:

The money will be nice while you make it and at least you will have benefits, like health insurance, for part of the year.

Role Play

Pete:

I am looking forward to making some money. I'm never sick anyway, so insurance is no big deal.

Sue:

So you are telling me that you won't have health insurance?

Pete:

Well, No. I won't.

Sue:

I see. How many months of the year will you work?

Pete:

Five or six, depending on how good a year it is.

Sue:

At least it will be nice to have time off to do what you want the rest of the year.

Pete:

Well, I'll need to find some work during the rest of the year because I won't make enough in a few months to live all year.

Sue:

That's too bad, Pete. There always minimum wage jobs at Burgerville.

Pete:

Yes there are. But I've worked there before. I sure don't look forward to it again, but it is honest work.

Role Play

Sue:

The job sounds nice, but I prefer to have a permanent job that's year-round.

Pete:

That would be nice. Still, I make a lot of money per hour.

Sue:

I hope you will do better than minimum wage for the rest of the year and you won't need health insurance in case you get hurt or sick.

Pete:

Yeah. Me, too.

Sue:

I've been trying for a job with Ace Company. It doesn't pay as much as your job by the hour but it's year-round and pays enough money so that I can live pretty well.

Pete:

Do you get benefits?

Sue:

Sure. I get health and dental insurance plus they have a retirement plan I can get started in when I've been there a year. I also get paid vacation!

Pete:

Paid vacation?! That sounds really good. Retirement? Health benefits?

Sue:

Yep. All of that and permanent work, too.

Role Play

Pete:

Hey, Sue. Do you think they have any openings?

Sue:

Why, Pete? I thought you were excited about your job.

Ask the class to help complete the blanks:

Pete:

I was but I would like a _____ job, with _____, that pays a _____ wage.

Chapter Four

Applying for a Job

Teacher's Guide

Learning About a Job

Purpose:
To introduce students to methods of learning about potential positions.

Objectives:
The student will

1. Recite resources for learning about open positions at a particular company.
2. Question employers to collect needed information.
3. List sources of information.

Procedures:

1. Introduce lesson by discussing that serious job search includes advanced preparation. An applicant needs to learn everything possible about the job. Methods for accessing information include:

   a). Talking to the manager and/or employees of the company.

   b). Asking questions when obtaining the application for employment.

   c). Checking with local organizations.

   d). Reading the job description

2. Select students to be role players.
3. Conduct role play.
4. Follow discussion suggestions.
5. Complete the worksheet.

Discussion suggestions:

1. Why is it important to learn about a company before accepting employment?
2. What is it important to learn about an available position?

Enrichment:
Invite the manager of a local business in to class to discuss what he or she would be impressed with in an applicant.

Worksheet:
Learning About a Job

Worksheet

Learning About a Job
Place a check mark in front of sources of information
that were presented in the role play.

_____ friend

_____ a relative of a friend

_____ a company employee

_____ a former company employee

_____ a customer of the company

_____ Chamber of Commerce

_____ Better Business Bureau

_____ the manager of the company

_____ the mayor of the city

_____ read a job description

Role Playing

Learning About a Job
Scene:

Andy has learned about a job opening. He is discussing the potential position with two of his friends, Tim and Allen.

Andy:

Did you guys hear about the stock person job at the market by the school?

Allen:

No. I must have missed it.

Tim:

My aunt works as a clerk there and I didn't hear about it, either.

Andy:

The job is for a stock person, but I'm not sure what they do.

Tim:

Maybe you would like to ask my aunt.

Allen:

I learned in career education that you need to know as much about the job as possible before you apply and interview.

Andy:

Yes, I really would like to know what my hours would be and what exactly the advertisement means by 'stock person.'

Tim:

You might also like to know the pay, what you need to wear, and the training that's required.

Role Playing

Allen:

Well, the store where my brother works, the stock person's put the stuff on the shelves and they work shifts of 24 hours a day.

Andy:

Do they have to work on the cash register? I don't have any experience at that!

Allen:

I think you need to ask the manager for a job description when you get the job application.

Tim:

Then you could ask my aunt about stock persons.

Allen:

Asking is probably the best idea. There's no reason for us to be guessing.

Andy:

You're right! I can't decide if I want the job unless I find out about the job, duties, benefits, pay, and all the details.

Allen:

Don't forget that you will be able to find out a lot of information during the interview, too.

Andy:

You're right. I remember a list of questions we got from career class that I can ask during the interview.

Tim:

Make sure you know when the deadline is for applying.

Role Playing

Allen:

Right. It would not be helpful to start applying by being late!

Andy:

It would be nice to know if their employees are happy.

Tim:

No joke. It could be hard to work for a company where everyone was upset. But that's something that you could ask my aunt about that.

Andy:

I was talking with Sue and she suggested I talk with the state Department of Labor to see if there have been labor complaints against the company.

Allen:

That wouldn't hurt, either. The more you find out, the better you will be able to make a good impression.

Tim:

How many stock persons do they employ?

Andy:

I'm not sure. Why?

Tim:

If they have several, maybe you could get a permanent job after high school.

Allen:

That would sure beat working at Burgerville!

Role Playing

Andy:

Maybe I can find out before the interview. If not, I certainly will ask during the interview.

Tim:

Andy, now do you have some ideas about what to find out and where to look?

Andy:

Yeah! Thanks a lot for helping. See you later.

Allen:

Good luck!

Teacher's Guide

Learning About a Company

Purpose:

To introduce students to the notion that the quality of the company is an important aspect for successful employment.

Objectives:

The student will:

1. Recognize how the quality of a company will contribute to their own successful employment.
2. Identify several sources of information about companies.

Procedures:

1. Divide the class into two groups. Name a company (large or small, local or distant). Ask one group of students to list positive things about the company and the other group to list negative things. Point out that most all companies have good and bad things about them and that the issue is what is right for you.
2. Select three students to participate in the role play.
3. Conduct the role play.
4. Review with the class the essential points of what information may be important and sources of information.
5. Complete worksheet.

Discussion suggestions:

What may happen if you were to use only pay as a criterion for a job? What would be indications that a company "cares" about its employees?

Enrichment:

Ask a representative of the State Employment Office or a local company to speak to the class about the importance of the quality of companies, and, if possible, give some examples.

Worksheet:

Learning About a Company

Worksheet

Learning About a Company

What are some of the benefits that are commonly provided by companies (circle the benefits)?

baby sitting	free lunch
insurance	retirement plans
emergency leaves	vacation time
sick days	new TV

Which sources might you use to learn about a company (circle the sources)?

Better Business Bureau	financial statements
employees	former employees
customer reports gossip	

Role Playing

Learning About a Company
Scene:

Jan and Sherry are walking, talking about choosing a company to work for.
They run into Marci and the three women continue their discussion.

Sherry:

Hi, Jan. Are you walking home now?

Jan:

Yes, want to walk along?

Sherry:

Sure! I heard you were interested in being a laboratory technician.

Jan:

That's right. There are three companies in the area that hire lab techs.

Sherry:

Hey, there's Marci. Marci, want to walk along with us?

Marci:

Sure. Thank you.

Sherry:

So, Jan, I guess you will work for whichever company has an opening?

Jan:

Not if I can help it. I want to work for the best of the companies.

Role Playing

Marci:

Don't all lab techs do the same kinds of things?

Jan:

Yes, the jobs are similar, but companies may be very different.

Sherry:

What do you mean?

Jan:

Well the benefits can be very different.

Marci:

Wouldn't you just want the most pay you could get?

Jan:

Pay is nice, but benefits can make a lot of difference
over several years of employment.

Sherry:

You mean retirement and health insurance?

Jan:

Right. That and more. The benefits that a company provides are a clue to how
they treat their employees. I want to work for a company that treats their
employees well, and with respect.

Marc:

How would you find out about all of that?

Role Playing

Sherry:
You could ask people that work there.

Jan:
That's one way I'll try.

Marc:
Never thought about this. What else would you like to know?

Jan:
I would like to know the length of time people have worked there.

Sherry:
Sure! If the workers have been there a long time they must think they are being treated pretty well.

Jan:
That's right. The state Employment Office can help me with some of that.

Marci:
Maybe it would be helpful to know if their customers have been happy. The Better Business Bureau could be helpful in finding that out.

Sherry:
Good point, Marci! My uncle knows about stocks and big companies and he could tell you if the company makes or loses money.

Jan:
That would be important because if the company goes broke I would be out of a job!

Role Playing

Marci:

It seems that there is a lot to know about a company. And all I thought was important was how much they paid you.

Sherry:

It seems that a quality company is very important for a quality job.

Jan:

It is for me. I'm looking for a long-term job and career.

Marci:

So you will need to check all of the sources you can find!

Sherry:

You have a few. Former employees, current employees, the Better Business Bureau, profit loss statements, asking the company itself, and the state employment office.

Teacher's Guide

Completing Application Forms

Purpose:
To provide students with a convenient and effective way to complete application forms both at home and in company offices.

Objectives
The students will:

1. Know the meaning of "Master Application."
2. Identify ways to use the "Master Application" when applying for jobs.

Procedures

1. Ask the students how many can write out an application for employment. Allow them to show hands or simply self-report their responses. Then, qualify the answer with the following: correct spelling, accurate addresses, correct telephone numbers, accurate dates, all information complete, the completed form neat and readable.
2. Select three students to participate in the role play.
3. Conduct the role play.
4. Review with the class the essential points of the role play.
5. Complete the worksheet.

Discussion suggestion:
Are there other ways you can use to prepare complete neat, accurate job applications?

Worksheet
Completing Application Forms: The Master Application.

Worksheet

The Master Application Form

Complete the application. Get help from your teacher when you need it. Use the application to complete other applications at home or in company offices

I-Can Company
60 Able Street
Mytown, Anystate   00001

Name _____ MI ____ Date _____
          first   *last*

Address _____ City _____ State ____ Zip _____

Telephone Number _____/_____ US Citizen: yes_____ no _____

SSN _____-_____-_____

Veteran: yes _____ no _____ Type of Discharge _____

Position Desired   _____

Employment History:
(most recent first)

Company _____ Position _____

Supervisor's name _____ Years _____

Reasons for leaving _____

Company _____ Position _____

Supervisor's name _____ Years _____

Reasons for leaving _____

Worksheet

The Master Application Form continued

Education:

High school name _____ Year graduated _____

Type of courses _____

Vocational school(s) _____ Year(s) graduated _____

Type of courses _____

Community college _____ Year graduated _____

Major _____

Four year college _____ Year graduated _____

Major _____

Licenses or certificates:

1. _____ Date received _____

2. _____ Date received _____

References:

1. _____ Phone ____/_____

2. _____ Phone ____/_____

Role Playing

Completing Application Forms
Scene:

Two applicants for a position are in the personnel office of prospective employer completing application forms.

Nelson:

Your name is Donner, isn't it?

Donner:

Yes, it is. I know you, don't I?

Nelson:

Yes, we had the vocational classes together.

Donner:

I remember. Are you applying here?

Nelson:

I am if I can get this application completed.

Donner:

They can be difficult. I picked one up the day before yesterday and took it home to complete it.

Nelson:

Good idea! I didn't find out about the job until this morning and the deadline is in one hour.

Donner:

Don't you have a Master Application to help you complete this application?

Role Playing

Nelson:

No. I don't even know what that is.

Donner:

It's just an application form that is completed with your information so that you can copy it onto the company form in the office.

Nelson:

So if I had one of those I could just use it instead of filling out this form?

Donner:

Generally, companies want the information on their forms so you would have to copy the information onto their application.

Nelson:

What if the forms are different?

Donner:

They generally are a little different but mostly you need the same information to complete them.

Nelson:

I think I remember something about that in our vocational classes.

Donner:

Yes, it was all covered there. Why don't you go to the school and ask Ms. Mitchell?

Role Playing

Scene:
Nelson is at school talking with Ms. Mitchell.

Nelson:

So what we covered was that we needed a Master Application to take with us so that we could complete the job application in the company offices.

Ms. Mitchell:

Yes, that was part of it Nelson. When possible you need to take the application home so that you can give it lots of thought and be very neat and complete.

Nelson:

I think I forgot about these things.

Ms. Mitchell:

Additionally, you need to learn to spell the essential words.

Nelson:

I can do most of that but I get the dates and company name confused.

Ms. Mitchell:

Well, again, that's where you can use the Master Application. Use it at home and in company offices.

Nelson:

Thank you Ms. Mitchell. I'll prepare my Master Application and use it!

Teacher's Guide

How Can I Apply for a Job

Purpose:
To acquaint the students with various methods of applying for jobs; to increase their awareness about making good impressions at each contact with prospective employers.

Objectives:
The students will:

1. Recite four methods of applying for a job (in person, Internet, mail, telephone).
2. Demonstrate that calling the company for their preferred method of applying is good practice.
3. Be aware that each contact with the company is important for making a good impression.

Procedures:
1. Divide students into small groups. Ask each group to decide among themselves how they would apply for a job. Ask each group to share its ideas.
2. Select three students to participate in the role play.
3. Conduct the role play.
4. Review the essential points (objectives) with the students.
5. Complete the worksheet.

Discussion suggestions:
Identify the advantages of each job application approach. Which method of applying would they prefer if they were the employer?

Enrichment:
Ask students to call a list of companies and inquire how they prefer that applicants place applications for employment.

Worksheet:
How Can I Apply for a Job

Worksheet

How Can I Apply for a Job

Find the words that describe the ways to apply for a job in the hidden words below and circle them.

```
E  T  U  Y  E  W  A  Z  X  V  C  G  A
D  B  I  T  E  L  E  P  H  O  N  E  Z
C  Y  N  T  R  F  V  B  G  T  A  Z  W
R  H  P  R  F  V  C  D  E  W  S  X  S
F  N  E  E  R  U  H  G  B  V  C  D  X
V  U  R  W  T  P  C  W  D  G  T  E  M
T  J  S  Q  G  L  S  Q  C  B  R  P  I
K  O  O  P  B  O  D  A  B  N  D  L  B
A  I  N  T  E  R  N  E  T  J  X  K  V
S  J  Y  T  Y  I  F  L  H  I  Z  O  C
D  K  I  R  U  M  J  K  U  O  A  I  X
F  M  A  I  L  K  H  G  P  L  Q  L  Z
G  P  O  W  U  J  I  O  Z  X  C  V  Q
```

Role Playing

How Can I Apply for a Job
Scene:
Hillary, Cassidy and Marco are sitting in the cafeteria discussing the best way to apply for a job.

Hillary:

Wow, I need to find some work but I don't know where to begin.

Marco:

Why not begin at the beginning?

Hillary:

Very funny, Marco! I really don't know how to start.

Cassidy:

Do you know which companies you like to make applications for?

Hillary:

Yes. I got a list from the state employment office of four companies that could use my skills. They have openings now.

Marco:

You could go to each company and see the personnel people and ask to complete an application.

Hillary:

Just walk in and ask?

Marco:

That's the way I did it, but I didn't get the job.

Role Playing

Cassidy:

That's too bad, Marco, but that is an acceptable way. Particularly for the larger companies that have a full-time personnel staff.

Hillary:

What would you prefer, Cassidy?

Cassidy:

I would prefer to call them first, being sure to use very good telephone manners, and ask them how they would prefer that I file my application.

Marco:

That's really good. Some companies have web sites on the Internet and would prefer that you apply on the 'net.

Cassidy:

And some companies have certain hours they prefer that you come in to apply.

Hillary:

I would think small companies might like an appointment so they can make time to deal with an application.

Marco:

That's probably true. Then, there is always the mail. You could get an application by calling the company and then return it by mail.

Cassidy:

There are lots of ways. That's why I contact the company and let them say what they prefer.

Role Playing

Hillary:

Contacting the company gives you a chance to make a good impression.

Marco:

So what do you think you will do, Hillary?

Hillary:

Well, I will call the company and ask them. I need to use my best telephone manners. I also need to ask if they have a web site where I can get more information and maybe apply on line. And look neat and clean.

Marco:

Saying please and thank you may help, too.

Hillary:

Yes! Every contact is an opportunity to impress them with my ability and skills.

Teacher's Guide

Cover Letters

Purpose:
To acquaint students with the purpose and use of cover letters.

Objectives:
The students will:

1. State the purpose of cover letters.
2. Draft a sample cover letter.
3. Name three types of information that can be included in a cover letter (personal experience, awards/achievements, exceptional talents, statement of goals).

Procedures:

1. Divide the students into small groups and give the groups the assignment of writing a cover letter to accompany their application for employment. Do not answer questions about what a cover letter is, but encourage them to think about it and try to come up with something that seems to fit.
2. Select three students to participate in the role play.
3. Conduct the role play.
4. Review with the class the essential points.
5. Complete the worksheet.

Discussion suggestions:

1. How long should a cover letter be?
2. What is the advantage of always using a cover letter with an application?

Enrichment:
Actually have the students prepare a cover letter for a job of their choice.

Worksheet:
Cover Letters

Worksheet

Cover Letters
Following is information that is good to put in a cover letter:

Awards or special recognition you have received (in or out of school)

I could include: 1. _____ 2. _____

3. _____

Experience that is important but not requested on the application form.

I could include: 1. _____ 2. _____

Hobbies that enhance your ability to do the job.

I could include: 1. _____ 2. _____

Special talents that you may have.

I could include: 1. _____ 2. _____

Work goals that are applicable to the particular job.

I could include: 1. _____ 2. _____

Sample Cover Letter

Dear Mr. Employer:

Please find my application for the job opening that was advertised in the (name of paper) paper last Sunday (date). The job requirements and my skills and training seem to match very well. My goal is to become affiliated with a strong company where I can use my training and good work habits to the company's advantage. I have received perfect attendance awards two of my four years in high school and intend to have good work attendance as well. I have special training in exactly the position for which you advertised. I completed the training in the spring and was second in my training class. Additionally, I really do enjoy the work and look forward to becoming established in the career field. I am confident that you will find me well qualified for the position and I look forward to meeting with you in the near future.

Suzy Sharp

Role Playing

Cover Letters
Scene:
Three students sitting at a lunch table.

Monica:

An interesting thing happened yesterday when I applied for a job.

Sean:

What was that, Monica?

Lucy:

Don't make us guess, tell us!

Monica:

Well, I went to pick-up my application and there was an instruction sheet attached.

Sean:

You mean one that says to provide reference letters and things like that?

Monica:

Right. This one included a cover letter as one of the things that they wanted with the application.

Lucy:

I've heard of applications, references, providing licenses and certificates, resumes and other stuff … but never a cover letter.

Monica:

It seems like it must be a letter to explain things not on the application.

Role Playing

Sean:

I think that is what it is. I studied about it in career class but I can't quite remember.

Lucy:

Okay, but what is it supposed to cover?

Sean:

I'm thinking. I'll remember.

Monica:

If you don't I can always ask Mr. Careerly, he'll know.

Sean:

It seems to me that you were mainly correct, Monica. It's a letter to be presented with the application to provide more individual strengths.

Lucy:

So what should it include?

Monica:

I intended to include my training, goals and experience.

Sean:

That's the idea.

Lucy:

Isn't that already in the application?

Role Playing

Sean:

Some of it is, but she will be able to explain how her life experience will benefit her on the job.

Monica:

And it really is. I used to help my father using the very skills they want. There's nowhere in the application to tell them that because it wasn't employment.

Lucy:

Maybe you could include your perfect attendance, and the 'on-time' award you received last month.

Monica:

I hadn't thought of that, but they may be interested in proof of my attendance and promptness.

Sean:

They might be. Include it in the cover letter.

Monica:

The cover letter is becoming clear to me now.

Lucy:

Me too.

Sean:

Just include the things that show them that you are the person for the job.

Sean:

Cover letters are good to use even when they're not requested.
But, they shouldn't be too long, either.

Role Playing

Keeping a Job File

Purpose:
For each student to be aware of the need to maintain organization in the job search.

Objectives:
The student will:

1. Cite the advantages of keeping a job file (by keeping a record of all contacts, applications and cover letters to use as models for other applications, the student replaces the need to remember activities).
2. Identify the essential steps of maintaining a job file (setting up a folder for each application, placing material in the folder according to date, making notes of telephone contacts and follow-ups).

Procedures:

1. Ask the students in the class several questions about the recent past. Or, have the students write their answers. For example: What did you have for dinner the day before yesterday? What was the leading news story last week? What place did the football (basketball, volleyball, baseball, etc.) team finish last season?
2. Select two students to participate in the role play.
3. Conduct the role play.
4. Review the essential points of the role play with the class.
5. Complete the worksheet.

Discussion suggestions:

1. Would being organized assist in getting a job?
2. What could happen if you forgot to do something in the application process?

Enrichment:
Have students that are applying for jobs maintain a Job File.

Worksheet:
Keeping a Job File

Note: This worksheet may be kept by the student as a checklist for maintaining their job file.

Worksheet

Keeping a Job File

Place a check in front of items that could be kept in a Job File.

_____ Job Application (copy)

_____ Cover Letter (copy)

_____ Letters of Reference (copy)

_____ School Records (copy)

_____ Licenses or Certificates (copy)

_____ Letters from the company

_____ Notes about telephone calls with the company

_____ Follow-up notes to the company (copy)

Other:

_____

_____

_____

_____

_____

Role Playing

Keeping a Job File
Scene:
Two friends, Carl and Manuel, are talking at a park.

Carl:
I'm so confused, I can't keep anything straight.

Manuel:
What are you talking about?

Carl:
My job search.

Manuel:
Isn't it going well?

Carl:
I think it's going all right, but I get confused about where I've applied, what response I've had, and what I put in which letters and applications.

Manuel:
So you don't keep a job file?

Carl:
Who said anything about a job file? What is a job file, anyway?

Manuel:
For one thing, it's a way to keep from being confused.

Role Playing

Carl:

Okay, Okay, I give! What is it and how will it help?

Manuel:

Basically, it's just a file where you place copies of all your applications and materials.

Carl:

So I get a file folder and stick all of the stuff in it?

Manuel:

That would be one way. I think you can do a little better by keeping one file folder for each application.

Carl:

What exactly should go into the file?

Manuel:

The application, cover letter, letters of reference, all responses from the company, and records of any additional contacts you made as follow-ups.

Carl:

It sounds like a lot of work.

Manuel:

Not as much as you do now. File each item in the folder in the order they are dated. Then you can refer back to each item.

Carl:

So I could revise a cover letter used for one job when I want to apply for another?

Role Playing

Manuel:

Exactly! It saves time and energy.

Carl:

It seems every time I write a cover letter I forget something I wanted to put in it. If I were just revising I would have it all in front of me.

Manuel:

Now you're thinking! And you make a note each time you call them or they call you so you don't forget.

Carl:

Then, when I look in the file I will know exactly what has occurred for that application.

Manuel:

Yes! Telephone calls, letters, the application, the cover letter, and every other contact with their office will be in the file.

Carl:

Now I understand why I am so confused! I try to remember all of that information without a file.

Manuel:

Feel better now?

Carl:

Like a new person. Thank you, Manuel.

Chapter
Five

Interviewing
for a Job

Teacher's Guide

Planning What to Say

Purpose:
To teach students the importance of planning what to say before an interview.

Objectives:
The student will:

1. Plan what to say before arriving at an interview.
2. Understand that knowing what to say will make a good impression.

Procedures:

1. Introduce the idea of making a good impression by discussing the need for being prepared. That includes knowing about the company, the job, and preparing to answer some standard questions. Allow the students to brainstorm about some of the things they will need to say during the interview.
2. Select students to be role players.
3. Conduct role play.
4. Follow discussion suggestions.
5. Complete the worksheet.

Discussion suggestions:

1. Discuss why it is important not to monopolize the interview.
2. Discuss the concept of "idle chatter" and why this is not appropriate.

Worksheet:
Planning What to Say

Worksheet

Planning What to Say

Circle the ideas that will assist you in making a good impression during an interview. Most of these items will be told to you.
So wait until you're near the end to ask many of these questions.

Use polite language

Say please and thank you

Dress comfortably but nicely

Ask about the job duties

Listen carefully to what they say

Be sure to know the pay

Ask about the hours

Benefits (like bus passes)

Is a uniform required?

Are there dress codes?

What about advancement?

Role Play

Planning What to Say
Scene:

Amy has a job interview. She is discussing the interview with two of her friends, Tom and Alicia.

Amy:
Did I tell you I have a job interview next Tuesday?

Alicia:
Good for you!

Tom:
Are you nervous?

Amy:
Yes, I really am. I wish I knew what they were going to ask me.

Tom:
Knowing what to say is important. But listening is very important, too.

Alicia:
That's true! Why don't we try to think of some things they might ask at the interview?

Amy:
Great idea!

Tom:
They always ask the usual stuff like your age and grade.

Role Play

Alicia:

They might also ask you what hours you will be able to work.

Amy:

That would be easy to answer.

Tom:

You really should ask them some questions.

Amy:

What would be good for me to ask?

Tom:

Ask what your duties will be?

Alicia:

I would want to know the pay.

Amy:

I wonder if a uniform will be required?

Alicia:

You had better ask.

Tom:

You may want to ask if the hours are different each week.

Amy:

That could be important.

Role Play

Alicia:

Some companies give bus passes to employees.

Amy:

I can see that there a lot of questions and a lot of things to think about before an interview.

Tom:

You have time to get prepared, and we will help you all we can.

Alicia:

Ms. Henderson, the career education teacher, has a lot of information on interviewing.

Amy:

I know her. I can ask her for some advice.

Tom:

I remember she said that there were some standard questions that many employers ask in interviews.

Amy:

Wow! If I could get those I would really be prepared.

Alicia:

She is really nice. All you need to do is ask her.

Tom:

Don't forget your manners. Say please, thank you, and don't interrupt.

Role Play

Amy:

And, Sharon reminded me not to talk too much. She said to keep the answers short.

Alicia:

I think you have all you can handle, for the time being.

Amy:

You're right, but I will be prepared!

Teacher's Guide

Ways to Make a Good Impression

Purpose:

To teach students the importance of making a good first impression when applying for a position.

Objectives:

The student will:

1. Understand the importance of making a good impression.
2. Be able to demonstrate confidence and initiative at an interview.
3. List questions to ask about a company and an available position.

Procedures:

1. Discuss how a good impression is enhanced when an applicant demonstrates confidence, initiative, dresses well, shows appropriate manners, and evidence of advanced preparation.
2. Select students to be role players.
3. Conduct role play.
4. Follow discussion suggestions.
5. Complete the worksheets.

Discussion suggestions:

1. Discuss why it is important not to monopolize the interview.

Note: Guide the discussion to assist students in making the following points:

a). listen carefully. b). wait until the speaker is finished. c). respond to questions briefly; ask questions politely. e). use Mr., Mrs., or Ms. f). remain standing until asked to sit. g). use please and thank you. h). be positive. i). smile. j). don't monopolize the talk.

Enrichment:

During the school year ask individual students that have distinguished themselves to be interviewed by the group. Also, contact Human Resources experts from the business community to come in to class and conduct mock interviews. The students will then practice their interview protocol.

Worksheet:

Ways to Make a Good Impression

Worksheet

Ways to Make a Good Impression
Circle the things you can do to make a good impression.

Listen to the interviewer carefully

Answer questions briefly but completely

Wait until the speaker stops before you start

Use Mr., Mrs., or Ms.

Remain standing until invited to sit

Don't monopolize the conversation

Ask questions politely

Use good posture

Smile

Say please and thank you

Be positive not negative

Can you name two other things that make a good impression?

1. _____

2. _____

Role Play

Ways to Make a Good Impression
Scene 1:
Katie Taylor is going to her first job interview.

Katie:

Mom, I need to leave. I want to be on time.

Mrs. Taylor:

Yes, it would not make a good impression to be late for the interview.

Katie:

How do I look, Mom?

Mrs. Taylor:

You look very nice, and that's important

Katie:

Any last minute advice?

Mrs. Taylor:

Be positive and smile as you walk in the door. And before you leave thank the interviewer for letting you do the interview.

Katie:

How do I end the interview?

Mrs. Taylor:

Well, thank the interviewer and say something like, 'I'll look forward to hearing from you. I know I can do a good job.'

Role Play

Katie:

That sounds good. I can do that!.

Scene 2:
*Katie arrives at the interview. She greets the receptionist
and is shown to Mr. Weston's office.*
Katie (She stands up straight and smiles as she enters):

Katie:

Hello, Mr. Weston. I'm Katie. I've been looking forward to this interview.

*(Katie remains standing. Mr. Weston offers to shake hands and
Katie shakes his hand firmly while maintaining eye contact.)*

Mr. Weston:

Please sit down and begin by telling me a little about yourself.

Katie:

I've been taking business courses and have had experience at Zoolo Company
doing pretty much the duties you are requesting.

Mr. Weston:

Excellent! What would you like to know?

Katie:

I'm interested in a career. Are there career opportunities with your company?

Mr. Weston:
Yes, many . . .

Role Play

(Katie listen quietly, maintaining eye contact and sitting with good posture.)

Katie:

What would the pay ranges be after a year or two?

Mr. Weston:

The pay would depend on what level you would start at and various other factors. Here's a sample sheet showing salary ranges and expected raises.

(Mr. Weston shows Katie a sheet of paper.)

Katie:

You have been really helpful for me, Mr. Weston, and I appreciate your time.

Mr. Weston:

Katie, you have made a good impression.

Katie:

Thank you, Mr. Weston. I'm excited about the company.
When might I hear from you?

Mr. Weston:

We will make our hiring decision no later than Wednesday.

Katie:

I look forward to hearing from you.

Teacher's Guide

Preparing for an Interview

Purpose:

The purpose of this role play is to prepare students for an interview by preparing answers and by practicing answers to the questions most frequently asked.

Objectives:

Students will:

1. Answer questions most frequently asked by employers.

2. List the three essential things employers are looking for in an employee.

Procedures:

1. Brainstorm with class what kinds of things an employer would want to learn during an interview. Write some of these ideas on the board.

Note: The three essential things they are looking for are aptitude, attitude, and attendance.

The seven most asked questions are:

1. Tell me about yourself.
   - What are your five greatest achievements?
   - How does your experience prepare you for this job?
   - Why should I hire you?
   - How flexible is your schedule?
   - Do you have dependable transportation to get to work?
   - What hours can you work?

2. Select students to be role players for prepared role play.

3. Conduct role play.

4. Follow discussion suggestions.

5. Complete the worksheets.

Teacher's Guide

Discussion suggestions:

1. Does the applicant have the aptitude or basic skills required to perform the job?

2. Does the applicant have the attitude or willingness to do the job?

3. Will the candidate have good attendance?

Enrichment:

1. Invite a representative of the state employment office to your class to describe what students need to do to gain and keep employment.

2. Take your class to the state employment office for a field trip.

3. Invite a local employer/personnel officer to class to tell students what they look for when hiring.

Worksheets:

Seven Most Frequently Asked Questions

Showing Aptitude, Attendance, and Attitude

Worksheet

Seven Most Frequently Asked Questions

Following are the Seven Most Frequently Asked Questions by Employers.
Write brief answers to each question using the guides.

1. Tell me about yourself.
   school, work experience, goals

2. What are your five greatest achievements?
   awards, sports, community service

3. How does your experience prepare you for this job?
   training, duties you did, work habits

4. Why should I hire you?
   good attendance, positive attitude, hard worker

5. How flexible is your schedule?
   be honest

6. Do you have dependable transportation to work?
   car? bus? bike?

7. What hours can you work?
   be honest

Worksheet

Showing Aptitude, Attendance, and Attitude

How can you show an employer that you have the needed aptitude (ability), attendance, and attitude? Use the guides below.

Aptitude *(having the ability to learn the skills needed or having the skills needed)*:

Specific training courses *(list any training)*:

_____

_____

Work experience *(list work that you have done which is similar)*:

_____

_____

Attendance *(being at work each day at the proper time)* Check the ones you would use:

_____ School attendance records

_____ Recommendations from other employers

Attitude *(cooperating, being part of the team)* Check the ones you could use:

_____ teams sports played

_____ school grades showing cooperation, work habits, attitude

_____ previous employers reports or letters

Role Play

Preparing for an Interview:
A sample Interview
Scene:
An interview room at a company.

Mr. Anderson:
Toby, this is Ms. Worker. She will sit in on our interview.

Toby:
It's nice to meet you, Ms. Worker.

Ms. Worker:
Toby, would you telling us a little about your background?

Toby:
Well, I'm a senior at ABC High School, and I'm interested in agriculture and I've participated in 4H and FFA.

Mr. Anderson:
That's a great deal of experience. What would you say are your greatest achievements?

Toby:
I consider my Grand Champion Award in Show and my Grand Champion in Confirmation of my 4H steer to be two of my greatest achievements.
Also, I received a Blue Ribbon in Public Speaking and I have gone to state in track the last two years.

Ms. Worker:
Those are impressive accomplishments for your age, Toby.

Role Play

Mr. Anderson:

Yes, that is an accomplishment. How do these experiences prepare you for this job?

Toby:

Well, I'm very comfortable in a competitive atmosphere. Many of the chores of 4H are similar to the duties you are asking for, and I enjoy being around people.

Ms. Worker:

Those are all characteristics that we would like our workers to have, Toby.

Mr. Anderson:

In your opinion, Toby, why should I hire you?

Toby:

I could do a good job because I have many of the skills you are requesting. Additionally, my attendance records at school are good, so I will be here. I have learned to work hard to achieve goals.

Mr. Anderson:

You are very impressive.

Ms. Worker:

How flexible is your schedule?

Toby:

Well, I'm in school until 3:00 for the next two weeks, but after that my schedule is very flexible.

Mr. Anderson:

Good. We need some flexibility.

Role Play

Ms. Worker:
Do you have dependable transportation to work?

Toby:
I have my own car, but it's kind of old.

Mr. Anderson:
How would you get here if your car wasn't running?

Toby:
I live on the city bus route so I could take the bus.

Ms. Worker:
You have thought of everything haven't you, Toby?

Mr. Anderson:
What hours can you work?

Toby:
I can work any hours you need me during summer vacation.

Ms. Worker:
Those are all of the questions we have, Toby.

Toby:
May I ask you some questions?

Mr. Anderson:
Certainly, Toby, what would you like to know?

Role Play

Toby:

Will I be required to wear a uniform? And when do I get my job reviews for pay increases?

Ms. Worker:

Very good questions. Yes, you will need to wear a uniform. We will provide it for you.

Mr. Anderson:

Job reviews are done after the first 90 days and then every six months. Pay increases are based on the reviews.

Toby:

I think you have answered my questions. Thank you for the interview.

Mr. Anderson:

We should be in contact with you by Friday. Thank you, Toby.

Teacher's Guide

Questions to Ask at a Job Interview

Purpose:
To provide students with questions they should ask potential employers.

Objectives:
Students will:

1. List questions appropriate to ask during a job interview.
2. Tell why it is important to ask questions of a potential employer.

Procedures:

1. Brainstorm with the class and list some questions that would be appropriate to ask. Select the best questions and write these down on the board.

Suggested questions include:

    a). How flexible is the work schedule?

    b). What type of clothes should I wear?

    c). Is there time for me to see where I would be working?

2. Select students to be role players for prepared role play.
3. Conduct role play.
4. Follow discussion suggestions.
5. Complete the worksheet.

Discussion suggestions:

1. Why is it important to ask questions?
   - to make an informed decision
   - show interest in the company/job
   - show initiative
2. Why should most questions be asked late in the interview?

Enrichment:
Students can talk to store managers or business people in the community about good questions for interviewees to ask during an interview. Students should report results to the class.

Worksheet:
Questions to Ask at a Job Interview.

Worksheet

Questions to Ask at a Job Interview

If you want to know something about a company, or a job, then you need to ask a question about it. What are some of the things you would want to know about a company or a job?

Circle the topics below you think are important to ask about. Then add some of your own.

pay

what they do

hours

how long in business

uniforms

training opportunities

benefits

company locations

travel requirements

pollution record

unions

promotion opportunities

_____

_____

Role Play

Questions to Ask at a Job Interview
Scene:

Ms. Johnson and Mr. Law are interviewing Andy Layton for a position at the company. Generally, job seekers ask questions at the end of the interview after the interviewers have had their turn. The interview has been going on for half-an-hour.

Ms. Johnson:

Where did you go to school?

Andy:

I went to the Main Street High ABC Job Training program and earned my vocational certificate.

Mr. Law:

That's interesting. What are you looking for from this company?

Andy:

A career with the opportunity for advancement.

Ms. Johnson:

That's a long term commitment.

Andy:

Yes, it is. That's why I'm interested in a company that provides training for employees. Do you do training?

Mr. Law:

Yes, we train current employees for both their current job and for advancement.

Role Play

Andy:

Does that mean that you try to promote from the current employees instead of hiring to fill positions?

Ms. Johnson:

Most often we do.

Andy:

If I started with your company what would I need to do to access training?

Ms. Johnson:

You would need to have the recommendation of your boss, a good attendance record, be a cooperative worker, and complete your current duties well.

Andy:

So I would need to be a good employee.

Mr. Law:

Yes. That is a nice way to put it.

Andy:

You mentioned that the company has several locations. Are there opportunities to move between locations?

Ms. Johnson:

Some jobs require travel and other jobs are used at each location so there is both the opportunity to travel and to move to a new location.

Andy:

That could be exciting.

Role Play

Mr. Law:
So you are willing to move?

Andy:
I've never lived anywhere but here but I sometimes think a move would be interesting.

Ms. Johnson:
That could help your career.

Andy:
Now, the benefits that you described, are they the same in all locations?

Mr. Law:
They are never less but sometimes there are more benefits.

Andy:
How would the pay compare?

Ms. Johnson:
About the same. Sometimes there are extras given if you move.

Andy:
I understand I need to be in the union here. Would I keep union membership if I changed locations.

Ms. Johnson:
Yes you would if you were still in a union position. However, managers are not union members.

Role Play

Andy:

How about my seniority? Would it continue?

Mr. Law:

Yes, as long as you are with this company.

Andy:

Thank you for all of the information and the interview. I'll look forward to hearing from you next week.

Ms. Johnson:

Thank you. Call if we can answer questions for you.

Mr. Law:

It's been a pleasure talking with you, Andy.

Teacher's Guide

Interview Follow-Up
Purpose: To show students the steps to follow-up a job interview.

Objectives:
Students will:

1. Send a thank you note to an interviewer after completing an interview.
2. Call interviewer a few days after the interview to check on the progress of the application for employment.

Procedures:

1. Discuss with the class what happens after the interview. Who does what and when? Let the students report what they think. Record some of their thoughts on the board for comparison later.
2. Select students to be role players for role play.
3. Conduct role play.
4. Follow discussion suggestions.
5. Complete the worksheet.

Discussion suggestions:

1. What is accomplished by the Follow-up to an interview?
   - a). Getting your name before the interviewer again.
   - b). Showing social grace.
   - c). Showing initiative.
2. What information would be important to impart in the Follow-up?
   - a). Your continued interest.
   - b). Your appreciation for their interest in you.

Enrichment:

1. Participate in a role play that involves calling an employer for a follow-up using dialogue generated by class discussion.
2. Provide each student with a copy of the follow-up letter to serve as a guide for them to prepare a follow-up letter. If you can provide actual practice of writing the letter in Language Arts it will enhance learning even more.

Worksheet:
Interview Follow-Up Thank You Note

Worksheet

Interview Follow-Up Thank You Note

_____
(your name)

_____
(your address)

_____
(city, state, zip)

_____
(date)

_____
(person with whom you interviewed)

_____
(name of company)

_____
(company address)

Dear :

I would like to thank you for the opportunity to interview for the position of _____
at the (name of company). It was a pleasure meeting with you and discussing the
_____ job position you have available. I am looking forward to hearing from
you soon.

Sincerely yours,

_____
(your name)

Role Play

Interview Follow-Up
Scene:

Ann interviewed for a job as a florist assistant last Monday. It is now Wednesday and she is calling Mr. Johnson, the florist with whom she interviewed. Ann dials the telephone.

Sales Clerk:
Hello, Johnson's Florists, may I help you?

Ann:
Hello, this is Ann Hoffman, may I speak with Mr. Johnson, please?

Sales Clerk:
Certainly, Ms. Hoffman, I will get him for you.

Mr. Johnson:
Hello, how may I help you?

Ann:
Mr. Johnson, this is Ann Hoffman. I interviewed with you on Monday for a position as a florist assistant.

Mr. Johnson:
Yes, Ann, I remember you. How can I help you?

Ann:
I was wondering when you will make a decision about the job?

Mr. Johnson:
I remember you and have your application here. You seem well qualified.

Role Play

Ann:

Thank you, Mr. Johnson. The reason I ask is that I have another interview tomorrow and that is why I'm requesting this information.

Mr. Johnson:

Well, Ann, we have one person to interview this afternoon. We can let you know this afternoon about 4 pm.

Ann:

That would be helpful for me, Mr. Johnson.

Mr. Johnson:

No problem, Ann. Thank you for calling and inquiring. We will be sure to call you.

Ann:

Frankly, Mr. Johnson, I would prefer to work at your store rather than the one at which I will interview tomorrow. I'll be looking forward to hearing from you.

Later the that afternoon

Ann:
Hello.

Sales Clerk:
Ann this is Sue, the sales clerk at Johnson's.

Ann:
Yes, Sue, it is good to hear from you.

Role Play

Sales Clerk:
Ann, we have made our selection and Mr. Johnson would
like to offer you the job.

Ann:
Sue, I accept the job!

Sales Clerk:
Good, Ann. Mr. Johnson is free now and would like to speak with you.

Mr. Johnson:
Ann, we are very pleased to have you with us.

Ann:
Thank you, Mr. Johnson.

Mr. Johnson:
Ann, you need to know that your manners, grooming, and your follow-up to the
interview were important things about you that we considered.

Ann:
I hope I did them all OK.

Mr. Johnson:
You did very well and that is why we offered the job to you. I'd like you to come
back in tomorrow.

Role Play

Ann:

Thank you, Mr. Johnson, I'll see you tomorrow.

Mr. Johnson:

I look forward to seeing you.

Chapter
Six

Expectations
on the Job

Teacher's Guide

Work Breaks: Breaks and Lunch

Purpose:
The purpose of this lesson is to introduce students to following a schedule, being punctual, and using appropriate facilities.

Objectives:
The student will:

1. Understand the necessity of having scheduled breaks and lunches for each employee.
2. Adhere to their scheduled breaks.

Procedures:

1. Introduce lesson by discussing:
    a). the need for a schedule for every employee at a work place;
    b). that schedules may change;
    c). an employee's responsibility for knowing his or her schedule.
2. Select students to be role players.
3. Conduct the role play.
4. Follow discussion suggestions.
5. Complete the worksheet.

Discussion suggestions:

1. Why do people need breaks anyway?
2. What should an employee do if he/she does not have assigned breaks?

Enrichment:
Divide students into small groups and allow time for each group to develop a schedule for an eight-hour shift, which includes two breaks and a half-hour lunch. Ask students to share schedules and discuss the complications that occur when schedules must be coordinated.

Worksheet:
Breaks and Lunch

Worksheet

Check three reasons for an employer to have schedules for employees:

_____ Because all employees can tell time.

_____ So that work can start at the same time.

_____ To make employees unhappy.

_____ To be sure that workers are ready to work.

_____ So employees will know what is expected of them.

_____ To allow the team to work effectively.

Do you need to know the following rules when you work?

Where to have lunch –   yes   no

Where to take breaks –   yes   no

When to begin work –   yes   no

When to return from breaks and lunch –   yes   no

When to go home –   yes   no

How to get a break that is not scheduled – yes   no

Role Play

Breaks and Lunch
Scene:

Paul has a new job. He is discussing what is required of him and his schedule with his supervisor, Tom, and another new employee, Allen.

Paul:

Hello, Mr. Olson. I'm glad to be here today. I came a little early so that I could get my work schedule.

Tom:

It's good to see both of you here this morning. It's good to plan ahead. You will receive your work schedules a week in advance, but it's always wise to check the board each morning for changes. You both can just call me Tom. We are quite informal here.

Allen:

Thanks, Tom. What are this week's schedules?

Tom:

Right now, you are both be in training so you will be working from 8 am to 5 pm.

Paul:

Tom, is lunch at a particular time?

Tom:

Right. Lunch will be from 12:00 to 12:30. Most employees eat in the lunch room. There is no food allowed in the work areas.

Allen:

The lunch room is where?

Role Play

Tom:

It is on your right, through those doors. There are coffee, tea, and cold water available for you as well.

Paul:

What if I need a break during working times?

Tom:

You will have 15 minutes at 10 am and 15 minutes at 2:30 pm. If you need a break other than that, ask your supervisor.

Paul:

What will be our usual schedule?

Tom:

After this week you both will be assigned to the evening shift that begins at 5 pm. You will, however, always have a half hour lunch break and two 15 minute breaks.

Allen:

The break times seem pretty strict.

Tom:

We have 300 employees and a production schedule, so it requires that everyone is ready at the same time. You will see that it works well for everyone.

Paul:

Can we change our lunch or switch with someone else during our shift?

Role Play

Tom:

That's a good question. We would rather the schedule not be changed unless there is an emergency or some other problem.

Allen:

What time should we get to work?

Tom:

We begin work at 8 am and expect that you will be at your work stations and ready at that time.

Paul:

That sounds pretty easy. Is there anything else we should know?

Tom:

It is important to be on time from breaks, too.

Allen:

Time seems real important.

Tom:

It is. If you are not at your station, then other workers may not be able to do their job either.

Paul:

Kind of like playing football. A team must start, stop, and act together if anything is to get done.

Tom:

Exactly. And it's time to start now!

Teacher's Guide

Appropriate Dress

Purpose:

To teach students the importance and the necessity of dressing appropriately for a job.

Objectives:

Students will:

1. Understand that appropriate dress is part of how others judge them.
2. Recognize that proper work clothing is part of the job.
3. Be aware that different jobs require different dress.

Procedures:

1. Introduce the idea that part of employment is to arrive attired for work in the manner expected by the employer and required by the job. Brainstorm with class different types of appropriate dress for different jobs. Record responses on the board.
2. Select students to be role players.
3. Conduct role play. There are several opportunities in this role play to stop and discuss the issues.
4. Follow discussion suggestions.
5. Complete the worksheet.

Discussion suggestions:

1. Does the manner in which an employee dresses reflect the employee's attitude toward the job?
2. Can the manner of dress affect the employee's ability to do the job?

Enrichment:

1. Discuss: Could an employee be fired for not dressing correctly?
2. Have students collect a variety of pictures of people from magazines. Ask students what they think the people in each picture are like. What job is the person in each picture dressed appropriately for?

Worksheet:

Appropriate Dress

Worksheet

Appropriate Dress
Place a check in front of the statements shown in the role play.

_____ Dress is unimportant for job performance.

_____ You could be fired if you do not dress correctly.

_____ Different jobs require different types of dress.

_____ Part of doing a good job is dressing correctly.

_____ For some jobs, safety is part of the dress requirement.

_____ If you are hurt while wearing inappropriate clothing your employer is still responsible.

_____ Clothing has nothing to do with work performance.

_____ Your attitude toward work is shown in your dress.

_____ It is your responsibility to dress appropriately.

Role Play

Appropriate Dress
Scene:
Toby shows up for work late and is not dressed properly.

Mr. Anderson:
Come in, Toby. Is there some reason you're . . . dressed like this?

Toby:
Well, I just overslept, Mr. Anderson. I stayed up watching the late movie and I just couldn't wake up.

Mr. Anderson:
I see. Is that why your uniform is all wrinkled and your hair isn't combed?

Toby:
Yeah, I guess so. I was going to get up and wash my uniform and get cleaned up, but I would have been even later.

Mr. Anderson:
Well, you'll need to go back home because you are not properly ready for work.

Toby:
Well, most of the time I am.

Mr. Anderson:
Toby, do you care about this job?

Toby:
Very much. And I'm almost always ready to work.

Role Play

Mr. Anderson:
True. But, Toby, the requirement is to be ready for work each day at the time you're scheduled.

Discussion point:
What else could Mr. Anderson have done with Toby?

Toby:
I'm just like everybody else, Mr. Anderson. I definitely need the money. I just overslept, that's all.

Mr. Anderson:
Well, Toby, I expect my employees to arrive on time, work hard, and be dressed in a neat and clean uniform every day!

Toby:
Well, this won't happen again. I'm ready to start work right now if you'll give me another chance.

Mr. Anderson:
Safety is an issue, too. Would you be safe in those shoes and having no gloves?

Toby:
For just one day maybe I could not wear boots.
And maybe I can borrow some gloves.

Mr. Anderson:
If you're hurt who do you think will be responsible, Toby?

Role Play

Toby:
Me, I guess.

Mr. Anderson:
Wrong. I'm the one who's responsible for the safe working conditions of my employees. That's why boots and gloves are required.

Toby:
I guess I didn't know that.

Discussion point:
How can clothes relate to safety?

Toby:
I used to wear these shoes at the store where I worked.

Mr. Anderson:
That was then, for that job. This is a different job. Safety requires boots.

Toby:
No, problem, Mr. Anderson. I got it.

Mr. Anderson:
If you were a new employee, Toby, you might not get a second chance.

Toby:
I understand, Mr. Anderson.

Mr. Anderson:
Be here tomorrow ready for work!

Role Play

Toby:
I will be here dressed correctly, on time, and ready to work hard.

Mr. Anderson:
With boots and gloves?

Toby:
You got it, Mr. Anderson!

Teacher's Guide

Minding Your Own Business

Purpose:

The purpose of this lesson is to provide students with insights about when it's appropriate or inappropriate to get involved in activities or discussions in the workplace.

Objectives:

Students will:

1. Identify when to remain out of an issue.
2. Identify when an issue involves them.

Procedures:

1. Ask the students to identify which of the following situations they believe they should become involved in, and those which they should not become involved in.

• A friend of theirs has a fight with his/her boy/girl friend.

• Their parents are having a discussion about who to vote for in the upcoming election.

• A person they do not know picks his/her nose in public.

• The teacher makes a mistake on their test paper.

• They are marked absent but were present.

Allow students some latitude with the answers. Guide the discussion to the principle that there are some things that are your concern and some things that are not your concern.

2. Select students to be role players for prepared role play.

3. Conduct role play.

4. Follow discussion suggestions.

5. Complete the worksheet.

Teacher's Guide

Discussion suggestions:

Scene 1:

    a). What don't Shelly and Archie know about the situation they are viewing?

    b). Is Archie being influenced to do something he would rather not do?

Scene 2:

    a). Would Shelly and Archie have been helpful or hurtful to Sam if they had told him the rumor?

    b). Was the issue of the rumor important to Archie and Shelly?

General discussion:

1. What happens if you get involved in issues that are not your concern?

2. What would a general guiding principle be for getting involved?

Enrichment:

Divide the students into groups of two or three students. Ask them to think about personal guiding principles for determining if they should become involved in an issue or not become involved. Have the groups share their personal ideas.

Worksheet

Minding Your Own Business

Worksheet

Minding Own Business

Check the statements that indicate that you have a real interest in the issue.

_____ The issue directly affects you.

_____ The issue is something you have an opinion about.

_____ The issue is essential to your safety.

_____ The issue affects your ability to do a good job.

_____ The issue is important for some friends but not for you .

_____ The issue is unpleasant, but you don't know the whole story, or what lead up to what you saw/heard.

_____ What is being done is different than you would do it.

_____ The issue is just a rumor at this point.

_____ The issue may be true but is not work-related.

_____ The issue is a personal one.

Role Play

Minding Your Own Business
Scene 1:
Archie and Shelly are standing in the parking lot of a store and see a situation.

Archie:
Did you see that?

Shelly:
Yes I did and I don't like it.

Archie:
Me neither. That lady wouldn't yell at her child like that.

Shelly:
You're right. I sure wouldn't do that if I had children.

Archie:
She needs to be more respectful.

Shelly:
Why don't you go tell her so she will stop what she is doing, Archie.

Archie:
Well, I, uh, I don't know.

Shelly:
Go on Archie. You know it isn't right!

Archie:
But, Shelly, I ...

Role Play

Shelly:

You what Archie? Go on over there.

Archie:

Okay, I'm going. I'll straighten her out.

Note: See discussion notes for Scene 1 discussion topics.

Scene 2:

Shelly and Archie have heard a rumor about their company that involves a friend of theirs; they're trying to decide what, if anything, they should do about it.

Shelly:

What is with you Archie?

Archie:

I just heard that the company is going broke and that Sam will be the first to be let go.

Shelly:

Who told you that?

Archie:

Mary said that Pete told her and he works in the front office.

Shelly:

So what are you going to do?

Role Play

Archie:

I guess I could tell Sam so he won't be so surprised.

Shelly:

Is it your business to tell Sam a rumor that may not be true?

Archie:

I'm not sure.

Shelly:

At this point it's just a rumor. And to tell Sam or anyone else just spreads information that may not even be true.

Archie:

That's true, but what then?

Shelly:

Well, I always ask whether this issue involves me or not.

Archie:

Well, it is if I'm not going to have a job.

Shelly:

True, but the key word is *if*. And, is the rumor about Sam being let go your issue?

Archie:

Well, no not Sam, but I would like to know about the company. That is my issue!

Role Play

Shelly:
Sure it is. It's mine, too!

Archie:
Let's try to find out the truth.

Shelly:
Okay. Let's go ask Ron, our supervisor, about the rumor.

A short while later

Shelly:
I feel a lot better now that we talked to Ron.

Archie:
Yes. It would have been awful to tell Sam the rumor and get him upset for nothing.

Shelly:
The new owners will need all the workers if they are going to expand production like Ron said.

Archie:
Exactly. And for Sam that promotion to the design department will really fit his needs.

Role Play

Shelly:
Nothing like asking the people that really know what is happening.

Archie:
I almost got caught in Mary's rumor mill!

Note: See discussion notes for Scene 2 discussion topics.

Teacher's Guide

Asking for Assistance

Purpose:
To show students how and when to ask for assistance.

Objectives:
Students will:

1. Determine when it is a better choice to ask for assistance.
2. Ask for assistance when necessary.
3. Recite the three criteria for asking for assistance (unsure, mistake, don't know).

Procedures:

1. Brainstorm with class why it is better to ask for assistance than to make a mistake? Encourage answers of saving time, being right, learning new things, getting the job done right the first time. List ideas on the board.
2. Select students to be role players for role play.
3. Conduct role play.
4. Follow discussion suggestions.
5. Complete the worksheet.

Discussion suggestions:

1. In Scene 1, did asking for help save time?
2. In Scene 2, would it have been better to clarify the instructions rather than guess?
3. In Scene 3, what should Ann do now?

Worksheet:
Asking for Assistance

Worksheet

Asking for Assistance
Circle your choice of answers for each statement.
You may circle more than one answer.

1. The best time to ask for assistance is:
   after you have tried everything else
   as soon as you recognize you may need help

2. Asking for assistance can:
   make you look smart
   show you are trying to do a good job
   make you seem like a fool

3. If you do not ask for assistance you may:
   make a mistake
   get fired
   be embarrassed

4. If you find you have made a mistake you should:
   report it to your supervisor quickly
   hide it the best you can
   try to fix it without help

5. You should ask for assistance when you:
   make a mistake.
   are unsure
   don't know

Role Play

Asking for Assistance
Scene 1:

Ann arrives at work and sees Heather, her boss, stocking shelves.
She quickly punches in and opens register #3.
About 15 minutes later, the register jams.

Ann: *(to customer)*

Excuse me but this register has jammed and it will be a few minutes before I can check you out. (Ann tries to fix the register.)

Heather:

Any problems, Ann?

Ann:

I think I can fix it.

Andrew:

Good luck! I can never get them unstuck.

Ann: *(to customer)*

It will just be another moment. Andrew, I need some assistance.

Andrew:

I'm no help. Call Heather.

Heather:

Ann, what is the problem?

Ann:

It seems to have jammed and I don't know what to do.

Role Play

Heather:

It is not difficult. Just watch what I do.

Andrew:

I need to watch, too!

Ann:

That was simple.

Heather:

Yes. Now you know what to do when that happens. Did you see what to do, Andrew?

Andrew:

I did. I can see that serious damage can happen if it isn't done right.

Ann:

I'm glad I asked.

Heather:

Me, too. Because you asked, both you and Andrew learned something new that will help you in the future.

Scene 2:
Heather has asked Ann and Andrew to move cereal from one place in the store to another, and Ann has already started.

Andrew:

What are you doing, Ann?

Role Play

Ann:
Moving the cereal like we were asked.

Andrew:
We were asked to move it by the coffee.

Ann:
I thought she wanted it here and wanted us to stock the coffee on the shelves.

Andrew:
We should ask before we do it all wrong.

Heather:
It's okay. Just switch the two and it will be fine.

Ann:
I'm afraid that I've spent a lot of time doing this wrong

Heather:
Well, next time you should ask first.

Andrew:
It is nice to be getting it right this time.

Ann:
I would have been embarrassed to ask.

Heather:
And you feel good now?

Role Play

Scene 3:
Ann has just accepted a delivery that she realizes is short some merchandise.

Heather:

Was that Tom with our supplies?

Ann:

Yes, Heather, he delivered two dozen. *(Then to herself she says)*
But I should have counted them to be sure: 21, 22, 23.

Heather:

I'm glad he got here with them. We need all of them.

Ann: *(To herself)*

What can I do if there aren't enough?

Heather:

Ann, pack up 24 for Ms. Fitz.

Ann:

I made a mistake! We are one short and I didn't count them.

Heather:

I will call the company and get one more today. You need to check the orders
as they come in, Ann. No harm done this time.

Teacher's Guide

Using Appropriate Manners

Purpose:
To acquaint students with the impressions that manners have on other people.

Objectives:
The students will:
1. Recognize the importance of good manners.
2. Use appropriate manners in work settings.
3. Avoid the use of slang in the work place.

Procedures:
1. Invite students to discuss the idea of manners being situational and contextual. Is there one set of manners that is acceptable everywhere? Record student answers on the board.
2. Select students to participate in the role play.
3. Conduct the role play.
4. Follow the discussion suggestions.
5. Complete the worksheet.

Discussion suggestions:
1. How do manners influence your opinion of another person?
2. Can a person know more than one set of appropriate manners?

Enrichment:
1. Ask the students to observe news reports on TV and then describe to the class examples of poor behavior.
2. Ask students to observe behavior in stores, on the highway, and in school for examples of appropriate behaviors.

Worksheet:
Using Appropriate Manners

Worksheet

Using Appropriate Manners

Place a check in front of each statement that would be a good thing to do in the work place or during interviews.

_____ When introducing someone in the work place, it is a good idea to use Mr. or Mrs. with the person's last name.

_____ Standard English, not slang, is preferable in the work place.

_____ When standing or sitting you should lean against something.

_____ When talking with another person you should maintain eye contact.

_____ Terms like Please, Thank you, and You're Welcome are important in the work place.

_____ Listen carefully to understand what is being said to you.

_____ When asked questions answer them directly and briefly.

_____ Good posture makes a good impression.

_____ Clean clothing is a must for most jobs.

_____ When entering doors or halls, let others go before you.

Role Play

Using Appropriate Manners
Scene:
Chad and Clara are discussing two candidates who just finished interviewing for a job with their company.

Chad:

Now that the interviews are over, we have to make a decision between Sheri and Jeff.

Clara:

It's a lot easier to interview than make the decision.

Chad:

I know what you mean. Either of them could do the job.

Clara:

I agree. They have very good skills and training.

Chad:

We could flip a coin.

Clara:

Hey, not so fast. There were some differences.

Chad:

Just joking. I noticed some important differences, too.

Clara:

What did you see?

Role Play

Chad:

I saw the look on Mr. Chief's face when Jeff called him by his first name!

Clara:

That was something. I've been here four years and would not do that!

Chad:

And when the secretary offered something to drink he just said 'sure.'

Clara:

Then, when she gave it to him he didn't say 'Thank You', either.

Chad:

That would not make a good impression on our customers or other employees.

Clara:

Yes, but Sheri said 'A drink would be very nice.'

Chad:

And told the secretary how nice she was to bring it for her.

Clara:

When Mr. Chief reviewed his training and commented on how well he had done Jeff used the phrase 'Right on.'

Chad:

As opposed to Sheri's 'I've worked very hard for the training and skills.'

Clara:

I almost laughed when he was walking with that street walk down the hall.

Role Play

Chad:

Several of the other employees that saw him did laugh. I'm glad he didn't notice. Makes me wonder how customers would react.

Clara:

I sure was impressed by the way Sheri stood and walked. She would make a good impression with our customers.

Chad:

She had a lot of poise and grace. Seemed to add to her confidence.

Clara:

Her confidence would make our customers feel comfortable.

Chad:

I liked the way that she looked each speaker in the eye. I think that's something her co-workers would appreciate, too.

Clara:

It let you know that you had her full attention. Then, she would answer just the questions asked of her and not a lot of other stuff.

Chad:

Jeff would try to add other information to make himself look better. But he would have been better off letting his training and experience speak for itself.

Clara:

I agree. I think we may have an easier decision than we thought.

Role Play

Chad:

Yes, and it is almost too bad. Because if Jeff would have presented himself in a more appropriate way things might have been different for him.

Clara:

There is certainly more to hiring a new employee than I thought.

Chad:

There sure is. The job skills get the interview but the manners get the job!

Clara:

Then we agree?

Chad:

Yes. Sheri is our new employee.

Clara:

She will have a positive influence on co-workers and customers.

Teacher's Guide

Starting and Stopping Work

Purpose:
To introduce students to the procedures for starting and stopping work.

Objectives:
The students will:

1. Ask their supervisors about work rules.
2. Arrive at the work station ready to work.
3. Ask their supervisors for permission for any special situations.

Procedures:

1. Take a vote of how many students like rules. Then ask the students how the school would be if there were no rules. Allow sufficient discussion for them to realize that without rules there would be no school.
2. Select the students to conduct the role play.
3. Conduct the role play.
4. Follow the discussions suggestions.
5. Complete the worksheet.

Discussion suggestions:

1. Do work places need rules just as schools do?
2. How do you find out about work place rules?

Enrichment:

1. Ask a local business person to visit the class and talk about the rules that are in the work place
2. Ask students to interview some local business people about the rules in their businesses.

Worksheet
Starting and Stopping Work

Worksheet

Starting and Stopping Work
Circle the correct responses.

1. At your starting time you need to be:

    arriving at work

    at your work station

2. If you need an unexpected break you should:

    make it short

    ask for permission

3. If you don't know what is expected you should:

    ask your boss

    do your best

4. If you are given rules to follow you should:

    follow them without fail

    try to do something close

5. Most rules have:

    no purpose

    a good purpose

6. Rules allow everyone to:

    be stressed

    follow the same procedures

7. If you can't follow a rule you should:

    tell your boss

    hope no one will notice

8. Starting and stopping work times are:

    exact

    only guides

9. Following rules can make the work place:

    safer

    a pain

Role Play

Starting and Stopping Work

Spence:
Wow, did I ever get chewed out at work today!

Traci:
Late again?

Spence:
Not really. I got there at 8 am just in time.

Traci:
So what was the problem?

Spence:
My boss said I needed to be ready to work at 8 and I had to change into my uniform before I could begin.

Mona:
I don't get it.

Traci:
I do. Spence needs to be ready to start working at 8 – not just getting ready to work at 8.

Spence:
That's what he said. I guess I will need to get there earlier.

Role Play

Traci:

I had a similar problem taking breaks at work. I would leave on time then return at the exact end of the time.

Mona:

So you weren't ready to start working at the end of the break?

Traci:

That's right. It seems like a small issue, but I guess it adds up with lots of employees.

Spence:

There are a lot of rules to learn and remember. One person where I work got into trouble for coming in the wrong way.

Mona:

I'll bet. The place you work has all of the military contracts and it's high security.

Spence:

Right. And he came through the office and the security guards caught him and had to verify who he was.

Traci:

So getting to work on time and using the correct procedures can be an important part of being a good employee.

Mona:

Even parking is an issue. I parked in the wrong place and blocked a fire gate.

Spence:

If there had been a fire, that would have caused a lot of delay for the fire department.

Traci:

Maybe even lives could be put into danger.

Mona:

Okay, I got it. They had me move my car.

Spence:

It seems like there are usually good reasons for most of the rules. It's just difficult to foresee all of them sometimes.

Traci:

That's why Ms. Sams, in vocational class, told us to be sure to ask all of those questions when we are hired.

Mona:

One thing I remember is that we need to ask where to park and how to check in when we arrive.

Spence:

I've learned to ask about the time of breaks and lunch and where to take the breaks.

Traci:

It would have been nice to know that before getting in trouble.

Mona:

Another issue is what to do if you need an unexpected break?

Role Play

Spence:

I think you should ask your supervisor before leaving your work area.

Traci:

Right, don't just leave.

Spence:

From the other workers I learned that were some things you need to do before leaving for the day, too.

Mona:

Where I work we need to clean up our area and put away all of the tools.

Traci:

There's a lot to know. We need to remember to ask about the rules and procedures.

Chapter Seven

How Jobs
are Lost

Teacher's Guide

Job Loss: It Happens

Purpose:
To teach the students some of the classifications of job loss.

Objectives:
The students will:
1. Define the meaning of "quit."
2. Define the meaning of "laid off" and "let go."
3. Define the meaning of "fired."

Procedures:
1. Write the terms "quit," "laid off," "let go," and "fired" on the board. Ask the students if they know what the terms mean. Lead the discussion for a few minutes, then begin the role play. It is not necessary that the students accurately define the terms.
2. Select three students to participate in the role play.
3. Conduct the role play.
4. Review with the class the three terms.
5. Complete the worksheet.

Discussion suggestions:
1. What do you need to do if you are fired to keep from being fired again?
2. What are some good reasons for quitting a job?

Worksheet:
Job Loss: It Happens

Worksheet

Job Loss: It Happens

Write the appropriate term in front of each statement:

Fired   Laid off/Let go   Quit

_____ John was often late for work and lost his job.

_____ Sally was absent most Monday mornings and lost her job.

_____ Pete was offered a better job and left this employer.

_____ A big customer decided to switch suppliers and Frank lost his job.

_____ All of the work was completed for this season and Sharon lost her job.

_____ Reggie left to join the military.

Role Play

Job Loss: It Happens
Scene:
Two acquaintances meet at the state employment office and begin a conversation.

Meagan:
Frank, how are you?

Frank:
Not too good. How about you?

Meagan:
Same as you. Did you lose your job, too?

Frank:
Sure did! A week ago today.

Meagan:
I'm sorry to hear that. I lost mine about then, too.

Frank:
Did you get fired?

Meagan:
No, I was laid off because of a slowdown in the business.

Frank:
How is that different than being fired?

Role Play

Meagan:

I think fired is when you do something bad and they fire you for it.

Frank:

So what is the difference?

Meagan:

I'm not sure I know, exactly.

Scene:

An employment counselor is nearby and enters the conversation.

Counselor:

There is a big difference.

Meagan:

Can you explain the difference?

Counselor:

Sure. If you are fired then you did something that caused you to be released from employment. If you were laid off or let go it is generally not because of something that you did.

Frank:

What would a person do to get fired?

Counselor:

Anything that was not productive in the work place. Too many mistakes, not being on time, and not getting along with others are some examples of things people get fired for.

Role Play

Meagan:
How is the result different? Either way you don't have a job.

Counselor:
That is true, but it can make a difference getting or keeping the new job.

Frank:
So if I got fired I will not get a new job?

Counselor:
No, but you may have more difficulty getting a new job.

Meagan:
And, if you got fired there was a reason. You would need to learn not to do that again.

Counselor:
That is correct. If you don't learn you may lose the new job, too.

Frank:
What if a person quits their job?

Counselor:
Well, people quit jobs all the time. It is neither being fired nor laid off.

Meagan:
It seems that if you quit too often it would not look good to employers.

Role Play

Counselor:

That's true. New employers like to see that workers stay with one job for a long time and leave the job for advancement or were laid off.

Frank:

So what they don't want to see in your employment history is that you were fired or quit often?

Meagan:

It sure could look bad if you quit all of you jobs or were fired from each job.

Counselor:

If you owned a business and needed good workers, who would you hire? Workers that lost their jobs or quit often, or workers that stayed a long time at one place?

Frank:

I would want workers who stayed at one job and did good work.

Meagan:

Me, too!

Counselor:

Most often, workers that stay with one job make more money, get more vacation time, and can depend on their job. What will you do?

Frank:

I want to work steadily. How about you, Meagan?

Teacher's Guide

Getting Fired

Purpose:
To acquaint the students with the idea of work-related skills and why individuals get fired.

Objectives:
The students will:
1. Define the term "work-related skills."
2. Define the term "work skills."
3. List five "work-related skills" for which workers may be fired.

Procedures:
1. Review the contents and objectives of **Job Loss: It Happens** with students.
2. Ask the students to explain what kinds of behaviors they think could lead to being fired.
3. Select three students to participate in the role play.
4. Conduct the role play.
5. Review the objectives of the role play with the students.
6. Complete the worksheet.

Discussion suggestions:
1. Do people get fired for not being able to do the work? (Yes, but most are fired for work-related skills.)
2. Ask the students to expand the list of work-related skills (dress, grooming, on-time, call when absent, limit absences, short breaks, limit chat, arguing with others, following instructions, etc.).

Worksheet:
Getting Fired

Worksheet

Getting Fired

The following is a list of things that could get a person fired from work.
Place a "S" in front of the items that are work related skills
and a "W" in front of the items that are work skills.

_____ A worker works in an unsafe manner.

_____ A worker is late often.

_____ A worker makes frequent mistakes in the job.

_____ A worker fails to call when they can't be at work because of illness.

_____ A worker doesn't know how to do a task.

_____ A worker always has another idea of how things should be done.

_____ A worker wears inappropriate clothing to work.

_____ A worker spreads rumors about others at work.

Role Play

Getting Fired
Scene:
A very sad Fred is speaking with Jane, his good friend.

Jane:
So, Fred, they fired you?

Fred:
Right, Jane. It wasn't fair!

Jane:
What wasn't fair Fred?

Fred:
That they fired me. I told them I would do better.

Jane:
Better at what, Fred?

Fred:
They said that I was not at work a lot, that I did not follow directions, and that I argued with the boss.

Jane:
Seems like they should have warned you first.

Fred:
Well … they kind of did warn me a couple of times.

Jane:
How is that?

Fred:
Well, the foreman said I needed to listen and keep quiet, and the manager said there had been complaints from other workers about my attitude, and the time keeper warned me about being absent.

Jane:
How was the work you did do?

Fred:
It was good. They said it was good. But, I still got fired!

Scene:
Enters Ms. John's, vocational counselor.

Ms. John's:
Hi, Fred. Is it true?

Fred:
Yes, it is true. I got fired.

Jane:
But, his work was good, Ms. John's.

Ms. John's:
Do either of you know why most people lose their jobs?

Jane:
Sure. They mess-up the work!

Role Play

Fred:
Or, they don't know how to do the work.

Ms. John's:
Not so.

Jane:
Then why, Ms. John's?

Ms. John's:
It is what we call 'work-related skills' or behaviors and NOT job skills.

Fred:
Okay, but I don't get it.

Ms. John's:
What reasons did they give you for being fired, Fred?

Fred:
Being absent.

Jane:
You said it was for arguing too, Fred.

Fred:
Right.

Ms. John's:
All of those are work-related skills, Fred.

Role Play

Jane:

You mean that even if you do good work you may get fired?

Ms. John's:

That is correct. In fact, most people are fired for work-related skills. Even if they do good work.

Fred:

That is what happened. I guess getting along, listening, and being at work are real important.

Jane:

Only if you want to keep your job.

Ms. John's:

That is right, Fred. Employers can train the work skills or change your job so that you will be successful.

Fred:

Are work-related skills what Mr. Kim was talking about when he said a 'good attitude' was important?

Ms. John's:

Exactly, Fred. Employers don't feel that they have the time or energy to deal with a person with a bad attitude or bad work habits.

Jane:

So they fire them?

Fred:

Apparently they do.

Teacher's Guide

Lost Your Job . . . Not Your Fault

Purpose:
To assist the students in understanding some of the reasons why a person may lose their job when it's not their fault.

Objectives:
The students will:

1. Define "laid off."
2. Contrast "laid off" and "fired."
3. Cite two things they need to do if they are laid off in order to get a new job.

Procedures:

1. Ask the students to state what they think the differences are between being "fired" and being "laid off." Record their ideas on the chalk board and leave for review later.
2. Select three students to participate in the role play.
3. Conduct the role play.
4. Review the contents with the class.
5. Complete the worksheet.

Discussion suggestions:

1. Why would you rather be "laid off" than "fired?"
2. Who's to blame if you are fired?

Enrichment:
Ask an Employment Counselor from the state department of employment to visit your class.

Worksheet:
Lost Your Job . . . Not Your Fault

Worksheet

Lost Your Job . . . Not Your Fault

Circle the word or phrase that is correct for laid off:

Easier to get a new job	Harder to get a new job.
Your fault	Not your fault
Can return to same company	Can't return to same company
No unemployment	Receive unemployment
Recommendation from employer	No recommendation
You were often absent	Company moves out of state
You were often late to work	You were on time
The business burned	You started a fire by carelessness

Role Play

Lost Your Job . . . Not Your Fault
Scene:
Two friends and an employment counselor discussing Brenda's situation.

Mr. White:
So when they let you go they said that you could have a good reference?

Brenda:
Yes. They told me that my work was very good.

Amy:
How can they fire you and say your work was good?

Brenda:
I did not get fired. I was let go or laid off.

Amy:
So what is the difference?

Mr. White:
One difference is that she is immediately eligible for unemployment benefits.

Brenda:
I can sure use that.

Amy:
Could she get benefits if she were fired?

Role Play

Mr. White:

When a person is fired there may be some additional steps to take before benefits can be paid.

Brenda:

Also, I can go back to work at the same company if the sales pick up.

Amy:

They would hire you back?

Brenda:

That's what they said. I was laid off because I was the last one hired and not because my work was bad.

Amy:

That would not happen if you were fired because that means your work was bad.

Mr. White:

That is true. Also, Brenda will be able to get another job easier because she has a good recommendation from her previous employer.

Brenda:

It would be much harder to get another job if I had been fired due to bad work or bad work habits.

Amy:

You would have a lot of explaining to do for the next employer before they'd consider you for a job.

Role Play

Mr. White:

That's true, Amy. And, for people who have been fired from several jobs, getting a job becomes very very difficult.

Amy:

What are the reasons people are laid off?

Mr. White:

Well, sales had dropped and they did not need as many workers.

Brenda:

I have a friend that was laid off because they got machines to do the work he had done.

Mr. White:

That happens sometimes. Another reason is the company may move to another state.

Amy:

It seems there are many reasons why people can lose jobs without it being their fault.

Brenda:

It seems so. I hope it never happens to me again.

Mr. White:

That's why it is important, if you can, to accept employment with an established company with a reputation as a good place to work.

Amy:

Companies like that don't lay people off?

Role Play

Brenda:

Not as often anyway.

Mr. White:

The good news is that Brenda can get unemployment benefits, will have the recommendation of her previous employer, and she has a good work history.

Amy:

It sounds a lot better than being fired.

Brenda:

It is a lot better than being fired.

Mr. White:

Now, Brenda, you need to begin making a list of companies in the area that use people with similar skills to yours.

Brenda:

And, I've already got my recommendations together and a resume prepared.

Amy:

You'll be working again in no time!

Teacher's Guide

What Should I Do?

Purpose:
To teach students a procedure to follow if they do lose their job.

Objectives:
The students will:
1. Compare and contrast "fired" with being "laid off."
2. State the first two things to do in a new job search.
3. Identify what they need to do if they were "fired."
4. Describe a "labor market survey."

Procedures:
1. With students in small groups, ask each group to make a list of things that they would need to do if they were to lose their job. Have each group share their list with the other groups.
2. Select students to participate in the role play.
3. Conduct the role play.
4. Review with the class the essential points of the role play. Then, compare the role play with their group lists.
5. Complete the worksheet.

Discussion suggestions:
1. Why are there extra steps to take if you were fired?
2. What is important about staying in the same career field, if you can?

Worksheet:
What Should I Do?

Worksheet

What Should I Do?

Place a number in front of each statement according to which you would do first, second, and so on.

_____ Make a list of possible employers in the area.

_____ Call the employers and ask if they have any positions on my list.

_____ Ask employers if they will accept an application.

_____ Make a list of job skills that I can do.

_____ Tell friends that I am looking for a job.

_____ Apply with the state employment office.

Role Play

What Should I Do?
Scene:
Two students and an employment counselor talking in an office.

Mark:

I'm not sure what I should do now that I have lost my job.

Ms. Rich:

That depends on what you need and want.

Joyce:

I'm not sure either.

Ms. Rich:

First, do you want another job?

Mark:

Of course! I need to work.

Joyce:

Me too!

Ms. Rich:

Mark, was your work record good?

Mark:

Yes, very good. The company was bought by another company and they let several workers go.

Role Play

Joyce:

I got fired for not being on time and being absent.

Ms. Rich:

Well, you both want to work but have different situations.

Mark:

I just want to get another job.

Ms. Rich:

You both may be able to begin a search, but Joyce, you will have some thinking to do.

Joyce:

I will?

Ms. Rich:

Yes. You need to identify what caused you to be late and absent, how you can correct that problem, and how you will convince a new employer that you will be there and on time.

Joyce:

I have some ideas and I'm sure that it will not happen again.

Ms. Rich:

Good, you need to understand what happened. We can go over that later.

Mark:

So I should begin a new job search?

Role Play

Ms. Rich:
Yes, Mark. A good place to start is with a list of jobs that you can do.

Joyce:
And then we need to make a list of employers that may hire workers for those jobs?

Mark:
I've got five job skills that I can do. I had some experience at my last job.

Ms. Rich:
That is a good start. Then you will need to identify employers in the area, like Joyce said.

Joyce:
Aren't these the first steps of a labor market survey?

Ms. Rich:
Yes, Joyce. Do either of you remember the next steps?

Mark:
Yes. I will need to call each employer and ask if they have these jobs and if they're hiring.

Joyce:
And we need to ask if they will accept an application for any of the jobs.

Ms. Rich:
Very good. You both recall a lot from the employment unit that you studied in career class.

Role Play

Mark:

We need to apply with the state employment office, too.

Joyce:

And check the paper daily, too!

Ms. Rich:

Don't forget to let all of your friends know that you are looking for work.

Mark:

I remember that that is called networking. It's a very good way
to find new work.

Ms. Rich:

Yes, it is. But try to get one of the jobs on your list. You have transferable skills
for that job and will have a better chance to get a good job that builds on your
skills.

Joyce:

If I remember right, a good job is one that's full-time and
has benefits like insurance.

Mark:

Don't forget that it needs to pay a living wage, too.

Ms. Rich:

You two are off to a good start. And Joyce, we need to talk.

Teacher's Guide

Developing a Job Search Plan

Purpose:
To learn the major approaches used in a job search.

Objectives:
The students will:

1. State five methods of seeking employment.
2. Describe each of the five methods named.
3. Organize the search into a logical approach.

Procedures:

1. With the students in group, brainstorm ways they think they could get a job. Record their responses on the chalkboard and save for use during the discussion.
2. Select three students to participate in the role play.
3. Conduct the role play.
4. Discuss the major points of the role play
5. Complete the worksheet.

Discussion suggestions:

1. Which approach to finding a job is the most successful?
2. How should you organize for the job search so that you keep track of your activities and job leads?

Worksheet:
Developing a Job Search Plan

Worksheet

Developing a Job Search Plan

Place an X in front of each statement that is likely to result in finding a job.

_____ Watching television

_____ Reading the classified ads in the newspaper

_____ Send out lots of applications to all sorts of companies

_____ Tell friends that you are looking for work

_____ Place an ad in the newspaper saying you want a job

_____ Use the internet to check company web sites

_____ Take two naps each day

_____ Check with the state employment office

_____ Call companies to see if they use your skills

_____ Buy a new car

_____ Stop in at local businesses and ask if they have openings

Role Play

Developing a Job Search Plan
Scene:
Two seniors discussing plans with their transition teacher.

Gene:

Ms. Ford, Annette and I will be graduating and we're not sure how to go about finding a good job.

Ms. Ford:

I'm impressed that you're so concerned about such an important issue.

Annette:

What steps should we take?

Ms. Ford:

What have you done so far?

Gene:

Well, I finished the welding program and am taking the certification test next week.

Annette:

I'm finishing the retail clerk program and will have my certificate at the end of the school year.

Ms. Ford:

Very good! You have both decided on a career field and have gotten the training to begin work in that field. Good start!

Gene:

I thought that I would apply at all of the companies around here.

Role Play

Ms. Ford:

Do all of the companies use welders? And are they hiring
if they do use welders?

Gene:

I'm not sure. Maybe I should call the companies and ask if they hire welders
and see what the hiring outlook is.

Ms. Ford:

That would help.

Annette:

That way you would only apply to companies where there's hope of
getting a job.

Gene:

Good point. You could do the same thing, Annette.

Ms. Ford:

You should both use the state employment office. Employers notify them when
they need workers.

Annette:

I knew they gave out unemployment. I didn't realize they could
help you get a job.

Ms. Ford:

Yes, and it's free! They also know the outlook for employment in each field and
who's most likely to be hiring.

Role Play

Gene:

So let me see if I understand. I should contact companies to find out if they use welders and if they will be hiring. Also, I should contact the state employment office to see if they can help me.

Annette:

What about using the newspaper and telling friends you're looking for work?

Ms. Ford:

Good, Annette. You should begin checking the newspaper want ads each day and you should make a list of friends that may be able to refer you for a job.

Gene:

I made a list of people and included some of my father's friends because they're managers and foremen.

Ms. Ford:

Good! It's helpful to have people on your list that can really help in getting a job.

Annette:

Is there anything else?

Ms. Ford:

You can always go door to door and ask if they need anyone.

Gene:

That would be one way to be the first to apply for a job.

Annette:

Yes, and if they had no job they might know who does.

Role Play

Ms. Ford:

One other way. The Internet. Many companies have online sites and they list job openings there.

Gene:

Wow, I can shop for a job from a computer.

Annette:

We have a lot of things to keep us busy.

Gene:

Right. We need to check with the state employment office and call companies to inquire.

Annette:

We need to tell our friends that we're looking for a job, and also check the newspapers each day.

Gene:

We can also go directly into a business and ask, or we can get on the Internet. We have a lot to do.

Annette:

I think I will make a chart to keep track of my efforts.

Ms. Ford:

Good. Organization is very important!

Chapter Eight

Changing Jobs

Teacher's Guide

Why Change Jobs?

Purpose:
To provide students with reasons and a format by which they may change jobs.

Objectives:
The students will:

1. State three good reasons for changing jobs.
2. Identify the advantages of staying with the old job until they have a new job.

Procedures:

1. With students in a group, ask them to brainstorm about the correct way to changes jobs. Guide them to a conclusion about the procedure they would follow.
2. Select three students to participate in the role play.
3. Conduct the role play.
4. Review the essential points of the role play with the students.
5. Complete the worksheet.

Discussion suggestions:

1. Why would new employers rather have you working than being unemployed?
2. What would justify quitting immediately?

Worksheet:
Why Change Jobs?

Note: The worksheet goes beyond the content of the role play and the students may need some assistance.

Worksheet

Why Change Jobs?

One reason to change jobs would be working conditions.
Circle the items below that would be part of your working conditions.

dim light   old desk

skinny boss   unsafe tools

harassment   dirty air

high standards

Other:

_____

What things would you want to consider when comparing jobs.
Circle your choices.

benefits   work times

hours per week   opportunity

permanence   attitudes of workers

turnover of workers

Other:

_____

Role Play

Why Change Jobs?
Scene:
Three students talking about their jobs.

Ryan:

My job stinks.

Lyn:

I thought you liked your job.

Tim:

You always talked about it like you liked it.

Ryan:

Well, not any more. It was exciting when I first started, but now it isn't what I thought it would be.

Lyn:

So what has changed?

Ryan:

Well, the pay is not as good as they said it would be. The working conditions aren't good and the attitude of the workers is bad.

Tim:

Any one of those things may be enough to cause you to think about changing jobs.

Ryan:

Besides all of that, I don't think there's a chance for me to learn more and advance.

Role Play

Lyn:

That is too bad, Ryan. You were so excited about the job when you first got it.

Tim:

Do you still like the career field you're in?

Ryan:

I like it fine.

Lyn:

So you would want to stay in that field?

Ryan:

Yes. There is a lot more to learn than I got in vocational training and I still want to learn more in this field.

Tim:

Then, even if this job is not working out you have gained experience and that will help you.

Lyn:

You're unhappy with the pay, work conditions, and opportunity. Sounds like time to switch.

Ryan:

Yes, it is! I'll quit tomorrow.

Tim:

Hold on, Ryan. It's better to keep the job you have until you find a new one.

Role Play

Lyn:

Yeah, Ryan. Keep working hard so that you can get a good recommendation when you find a new job.

Ryan:

If I keep working there I can be real picky about my next job.

Lyn:

That way you can get just what you want and stay in the same career field.

Tim:

It looks better to a new employer for someone to be working than to be unemployed.

Ryan:

What I want most is the opportunity to learn more and advance.

Tim:

That will sound good to a new employer.

Lyn:

It shows that you have goals and ambition.

Ryan:

I will show my responsibility by staying with one job until I get the new job, too.

Lyn:

I think we have it all together. Stay with the old job while you look for the new job.

Role Play

Tim:

Have good reasons for leaving your job.

Ryan:

And, keep working hard until you have a new job.

Lyn:

He has good reasons.

Tim:

Yep! Money, work conditions, and opportunity.

Ryan:

It even sounds good to me. I'll begin my new job search tomorrow instead of quitting.

Tim and Lyn:

Good luck, Ryan!

Teacher's Guide

Change to What?

Purpose:
To encourage students to try and resolve conflict by asking for change before quitting a job.

Objectives:
The students will:

1. Cite examples of the types of work situations that may be resolved by asking for change.
2. Recognize that it is best to ask for change before quitting.
3. Recognize their ability to be a self-advocate.

Procedures:

1. Divide the class into three groups. Provide each group with a work problem (low wages, poor work conditions, no opportunity for advancement). Ask each group to determine how they would resolve the problem. Allow time for the groups to share.
2. Select three students to participate in the role play.
3. Conduct the role play.
4. Review the essential points of the role play.
5. Complete the worksheet.

Discussion suggestions:

1. Are there work problems that can't be resolved by talking about them?
2. What kind?
3. Why may a new job be no better than the old job?

Worksheet
Change to What?

Worksheet

Change to What?

Place a check in front of each work situation that may be resolved by asking.

_____ pay   _____ working conditions

_____ learning opportunities   _____ hours

_____ time off   _____ duties

_____ accommodations   _____ starting times

Circle the answer at the end of each statement.

Is it best to ask to solve the problems instead of quitting?
yes   no

Could a new job have just as many problems as the old job?
yes   no

Can you ask for changes and then quit if you don't get what you wanted?
yes   no

If you get what you asked for would you need to change jobs?
yes   no

Are there any advantages to being with the same company for a long time?
yes   no

Role Play

Change to What?
Scene:
Three friends discussing their jobs.

Loni:
I sure do want to change jobs. The pay is so bad where I work.

Bob:
Haven't you gotten raises for your good work?

Loni:
No. I thought I would, but there have been no raises and
I have been there two years.

Rich:
That's a long time without a raise. What do they say when you ask?

Loni:
I haven't asked. I just don't know how to begin.

Bob:
It seems that asking for a raise would be easier than finding a new job.

Rich:
Right. You always seemed to like the job and company.

Loni:
I still like the job and company. It's just that they don't give raises.

Role Play

Rich:

Why should you keep doing a good job and not ask for one?

Bob:

It would seem better to ask before you change jobs.

Loni:

I think you're right. How would I do that?

Bob:

First, you'll need to know how much your job pays at other companies.

Rich:

Be sure to find out how much it pays after two years of experience.

Bob:

Then you need to ask the person at your company who can make the decision to give you a raise.

Loni:

Wouldn't that be my foreman?

Bob:

Probably not. It is probably the manager or personnel manager.

Rich:

While you are asking, you'll need to learn their policy on raises so you will know what to expect in the future.

Role Play

Loni:

I remember that my cousin needed to ask for more opportunity to learn new things. She got what she wanted and is now a supervisor.

Bob:

Yes, asking will sometimes get anything you need.

Rich:

Right. It may get you better working conditions, more pay, and more opportunity.

Loni:

I guess if there is a problem at work you need to ask about it before quitting and finding new work.

Bob:

Very true, bosses can't read your mind.

Scene:
Loni leaves and returns in a moment.

Loni:

Guess what happened today?

Rich:

You won the lottery?

Loni:

Almost as good. I asked for a raise. I told them what other companies paid and they gave me more than that.

Role Play

Bob:

That's great. It pays to ask.

Loni:

They said I was a very good worker and they didn't want to lose me.

Rich:

I'll bet you will ask again the next time something isn't the way you would like.

Loni:

You bet I will. We also had a great conversation about what I wanted for the future. They'll try to give me chances to learn more.

Bob:

You really did well, Loni.

Rich:

I wonder what I should ask for?

Teacher's Guide

Staying in Your Career Field

Purpose:
To teach the students the advantages of remaining in a single career field.

Objectives:
The students will:
1. Recognize the multiple job opportunities within a career field.
2. Appreciate the transferable skills that are developed by staying in a career field.
3. Identify the advantages of finding a new job before leaving the current job.

Procedures:
1. Ask the students to name all of the kinds of teachers they can. Write the names on the board. When finished, draw a circle around all of the names and label the circle "teaching profession." Ask the students which is the career field and which is the job?
2. Select three students to participate in the role play.
3. Conduct the role play.
4. Review the essential points of the role play.
5. Complete the worksheet.

Discussion suggestions:
1. How can you tell the difference between a career field and a job within a career field?
2. How many jobs are there in a career field?

Worksheet:
Staying in Your Career Field

Worksheet

Staying in Your Career Field

List the jobs under the correct career field .

Jobs:

carpenter	store manager	nurse
nurse's aide	electrician	stocker
doctor	bagger	electrician
painter	receptionist	cashier

Careers:

Healthcare	Building trades	Retail clerk
_____	_____	_____
_____	_____	_____
_____	_____	_____
_____	_____	_____

Role Play

Staying in Your Career Field
Scene:
Three friends talking about changing jobs.

Dale:

I may need to find a new job.

Julie:

Still the same problems at work?

Dale:

I can't seem to get them solved.

Julie:

I know you said you were going to talk with the boss.

Dale:

I did, twice, but nothing has happened.

Ken:

At some point I guess you need to look elsewhere.

Julie:

Maybe that time is now, Dale.

Dale:

It seems like it is. If I look and find a new job I can talk with them once more, then leave if nothing happens.

Role Play

Ken:

What will you look for, Dale?

Dale:

The same career field. I like what I do and I have gotten a lot of experience.

Julie:

What do you mean by the same career field? You're an auto mechanic, aren't you?

Ken:

There are lots of jobs in a career field, Julie.

Dale:

Right. I started off as a helper, then a lube mechanic.
Now I'm a front-end mechanic.

Julie:

So what job would you look for now?

Dale:

It doesn't matter. Any job having to do with auto mechanics.

Ken:

Good Dale. Pretty soon you'll be able to do anything on a car.

Julie:

I see. So a career is a group of jobs that are related to each other.

Role Play

Dale:

Right. By staying in one career most everything I learn will be useful in more than one job.

Ken:

I remember Ms. Lucky. She taught 1st grade, 7th grade math, and 12th grade English.

Julie:

All in the career of teaching. Now she's a principal.

Dale:

It's the same way in mechanics. Each job builds skills that can be used in other jobs.

Ken:

So when you look for a job you'll have a lot of jobs to look for in the auto mechanic field.

Julie:

That way you have more chances and will be better qualified for the job.

Dale:

Mmhmm. I remember Mr. Good telling us that in transition class. I didn't think much about it then but now I am using the information.

Ken:

So where are you going with this?

Role Play

Dale:

First, I ask to change what is causing me difficulty. If I can't get it changed, I may ask again. If I get what I need then that's the end of it.

Julie:

Then, you look for another job and quit.

Ken:

No, he looks for another job and if he is offered the job he may ask again or he may just accept the new job and quit.

Dale:

In any case, I don't quit until I have the new job.

Julie:

Good planning, Dale.

Teacher's Guide

Quitting

Purpose:
To increase students' awareness that how you quit a job may influence your ability to get another job; to provide students with a format for quitting a job.

Objectives:
The student will:

1. Cite the usual length of notice for quitting a job.
2. Know to ask for a recommendation.
3. Understand that it is best to get a new job before quitting the current job.

Procedures:

1. Ask for volunteers from the class to role play quitting a job. Allow for two or three role plays. On the board make notes of the methods used. Save the notes for comparison with the lesson's method for quitting.
2. Select three students to participate in the role play.
3. Conduct the role play.
4. Review the essential points of the role play.
5. Complete the worksheet.

Discussion suggestions:

1. Why would an employer care if someone quits without notice?
2. How is it better for you if you thank the employer and ask for a recommendation?

Worksheet:
Quitting

Worksheet

Quitting

Complete the blanks in the statement below so that it describes the best way to deal with being unhappy with your job.

1. The first thing to do is to _____ to your boss.

2. If that doesn't work then begin a _____ but keep working hard.

3. When you get a new job give your boss _____ notice of quitting.

4. Then you may also _____ and ask for a _____.

Words to use:

thank them

talk

recommendation

two weeks

job search

Role Play

Quitting
Scene:
Three friends talking in the employment office.

Liz:
I had had it with my job so I quit!

Vic:
What was so bad, Liz?

Liz:
Mainly the pay and opportunities to learn more.

Marty:
What did they say when you talked to them?

Liz:
Talk? I didn't talk. I just quit.

Vic:
Didn't they ask you why?

Marty:
They must have asked when you gave notice of quitting.

Liz:
They never asked me anything because I never gave them a chance.

Vic:
What do you mean?

Role Play

Liz:

I just walked out one day and never went back!

Marty:

How long ago was that, Liz?

Liz:

About four months.

Vic:

You have been looking for another job for four months?

Marty:

That's a long time to be out of work.

Liz:

The employment counselor says I should have tried to talk with them. If that didn't work, then I should have given notice or looked for another job before quitting. But, I showed them!

Vic:

Right! You've been out of work four months.

Marty:

I'm unhappy with my job, but I talked with them and now I am looking for another job.

Liz:

So what did it get you?

Role Play

Marty:

I'll have another job before I quit and a good recommendation from my current job.

Vic:

And he might have saved his current job if talking with them had worked.

Liz:

So you two think that my four months of unemployment has something to do with the way I quit?

Vic:

It probably has everything to do with it.

Marty:

Sure. The places you apply will talk with your last employer to get a recommendation.

Vic:

Any guess what they will recommend for you, Liz?

Liz:

Okay, I think I see the point.

Marty:

I took a day off to come in here and register with the state employment office to begin my job search before I quit.

Vic:

When I changed jobs a year ago I thanked them for the opportunities they gave me. They were impressed.

Role Play

Marty:

Vic, did you ask for a recommendation, too?

Vic:

Sure! I got a good one, too.

Liz:

Maybe this changing jobs is not as easy as I thought.

Marty:

You need to try to solve the problems first.

Vic:

Then, begin your job search and give two weeks notice when you get a new job.

Liz:

Also, I need to thank them and ask for a recommendation.

Vic:

It may have saved you four months of unemployment.

Teacher's Guide

Comparing Jobs

Purpose:
To teach students that they need to compare jobs before switching.

Objectives:
The students will:
1. State the difference between temporary and permanent employment.
2. Identify the two advantages of full-time, year-round work.
3. Identify the type of benefits they would like to have included in their jobs.
4. Cite the types of opportunities they would like their jobs to provide.
5. List five questions they would be sure to ask about a new job.

Procedures:
1. Write on the board Job A and Job B. Beneath Job A write $13.00 per hour. Beneath Job B write $9.00 per hour. Ask the students to say which job they would rather have. Then under Job A write that it is temporary, has no benefits, and work hours are midnight until 9 am, Friday through Wednesday. Under Job B write that it is full-time and permanent, has full benefits including three weeks paid vacation, and work hours are 8:30 am - 5 pm, Monday through Friday. Then ask them again which job they would rather have.
2. Select three students to participate in the role play.
3. Conduct the role play.
4. Review the essential points of the role play.
5. Complete the worksheet.

Discussion suggestions:
1. When would temporary work be okay?
2. Are there questions about a job you should not ask?

Worksheet:
Comparing Jobs

Worksheet

Comparing Jobs

Place a check by each item that you would like your job to include.

After high school I would want a job that includes the following:

_____ good pay	_____ health insurance
_____ full-time	_____ no weekend work
_____ night work	_____ weekend work
_____ retirement plan	_____ paid vacation
_____ sick leave	_____ uniforms
_____ seasonal work	_____ advancement
_____ permanent	_____ other _____

*Now, go back over the list and circle the three items
that are most important for you.*

Role Play

Comparing Jobs
Scene:

Two friends are talking with one another when a third person joins them.

Ann:

Did you know that I've had a couple of jobs since I last saw you?

Ken:

No, I didn't know that. What happened?

Ann:

They just didn't seem to work out. Just the same old problems.

Ken:

So every time you got another job you found problems similar to the old job.

Ann:

Mostly that's what I found. One job was even worse.

Ken:

That's really bad luck.

Scene:
Enter the vocational counselor.

Mr. Nice:

Luck had nothing to do with it, Ken.

Ken:

Hi, Mr. Nice. What do you mean?

Role Play

Ann:
How could it not be luck?

Mr. Nice:
When you change jobs you need to compare the new one with the old one.

Ann:
I thought I did. My old job didn't offer any pay increases so I got a job with more pay.

Ken:
Seems like that should have solved the problem.

Mr. Nice:
Did it solve the problem, Ann?

Ann:
Well, not for long. After two months they shut down the plant for the slow season and I was out of work for three months.

Ken:
So you made more by the hour but less in the long run?

Ann:
That's right. To make it even worse, there were no benefits like health insurance.

Mr. Nice:
There are several things you need to be sure of before you change jobs.

Role Play

Ken:

That's for sure! You need to know the amount of pay and if the work is permanent year-round or not.

Ann:

That's right. It's hard to make enough in a few months to equal what you make with full-time work.

Mr. Nice:

Isn't there more that you want to know?

Ken:

I would want to know about the benefits. High pay without benefits may not be a good idea.

Ann:

The benefits I want most are health insurance and a retirement plan.

Mr. Nice:

Then you would need to ask about those and compare them to your existing job.

Ken:

And, do that before you quit.

Ann:

Another thing that's important to me is not working weekends. One of the new jobs required that I work weekends.

Mr. Nice:

So the days you are required to work is important, too.

Role Play

Ken:

Sometimes jobs are temporary instead of permanent. I want to be sure which the job is.

Ann:

I want an opportunity for advancement. Should I ask about that, too?

Mr. Nice:

If you want to know, you need to ask.

Ann:

So this time I will be sure the job is permanent and full-time.

Ken:

And, that it has benefits like health insurance.

Mr. Nice:

And don't forget about advancement.

Ann:

I'm prepared this time. No more mistakes in changing jobs!

Chapter
Nine

Vocational
Communications

Teacher's Guide

Interrupting

Purpose:

To introduce the protocol for interrupting the conversations, and taking the time, of others in the business workplace.

Objectives:

The student will:

1. Demonstrate gracious behaviors when interrupting is required.
2. Recognize the need to have an urgent need before interrupting.
3. Demonstrate similar protocols for persons that are superior or subordinate to their position.

Procedures:

1. Ask the students to list when it is acceptable to interrupt others.
   List some of the ideas on the board.
2. Select students to play the roles.
3. Conduct the role play one scene at a time.

After Scene 1, ask the class to identify what was done correctly. Responses should include that Ethan was brief, courteous, and concise. Note that because the interruption was in the normal course of business Ethan did not wait for Mr. Thompson to acknowledge him. This practice may not be appropriate for all supervisors or bosses.

After Scene 2, ask the class to identify what was appropriately done by those involved.
The conclusions should include that the call was urgent, Ethan was brief, Nike volunteered not to take the call (letting Mr. Thompson know that he was of primary importance at this time).
Mr. Thompson was gracious in suggesting that Nike take the call that was termed urgent (showing feelings for others' needs).

After Scene 3, ask the students to identify what was appropriately done by the participants.
The conclusions should include that the protocol is similar for subordinates to superiors, as well as the converse.

After Scene 4, ask the students to identify what could have/should have occurred. The conclusions should include that the signature was not urgent, Mr. Thompson was needlessly interrupted, and Ethan did not take no for an answer.

Teacher's Guide

Discussions suggestions:

1. Expand the discussion of when interruptions are acceptable.
2. Discuss how it makes others feel to be needlessly interrupted.

Enrichment:

Ask the students to look at their own lives for examples of interruptions, both acceptable and unacceptable, and have them report these to the class.

Worksheet:

Interrupting

Worksheet

Interrupting

Circle the phrases that indicate when interrupting may be acceptable:

you want it now   emergencies   the issue is urgent   the person asked to be interrupted

Circle the phrases that describe the best behavior when you need to interrupt:

take your time   be brief   apologize for interrupting   stop if told 'No'

Circle the phrases that indicate the general rules for interrupting:

be polite   be brief   be short   use respect   only for urgent issues

Role Play

Interrupting
Scene 1:
A business office with a receptionist, manager and a customer.
Customer, Nike, steps into the office.
Mr. Thompson, the office manager, is talking on the telephone.

Ethan (receptionist):
Hello, can I help you?

Nike:
Yes, thank you, I have an appointment with Mr. Thompson.

Ethan:
I'll let him know you are here. Please, have a seat.

Ethan goes over to Mr. Thompson.

Ethan:
Excuse me, Mr. Thompson, your appointment is here.

Mr. Thompson:
I'll be right there.

Ethan:
Mr. Thompson will be right with you, he's on the telephone.

Role Play

Scene 2:

Nike and Mr. Thompson are discussing business. Ethan is at the front desk working. The telephone rings and Ethan answers the telephone.

Ethan:

Hello, Arts Company … Yes, Nike is here but she is meeting with Mr. Thompson … I will ask for you. Excuse me Mr. Thompson and Nike, but there is a call for Nike and the caller has indicated that it is urgent.

Nike:

Would you tell the caller I will call them back.

Mr. Thompson:

Please, take the call if it is urgent.

Nike:

Thank you, I will be just a moment.

Scene 3:

Ethan and a co-worker, Liberty, are discussing some work.
Mr. Thompson comes into the scene and needs to speak with Liberty.

Ethan:

If we can do it all today then tomorrow we could move on with the main project.

Liberty:

Yes, that makes …

Role Play

Mr. Thompson:
Pardon me, Liberty, when you have a moment I would like to see you.

Liberty:
Certainly, Mr. Thompson. I'll just be a couple minutes, if that's all right.

Mr. Thompson:
That's fine, thank you.

Scene 4:
Ethan is having a bad day. Mr. Thompson is talking on the telephone.

Mr. Thompson:
Who is on the telephone, Ethan?

Ethan:
Ms. James.

Mr. Thompson:
Hello, Ms. James, I hope that you receive …

Ethan:
Mr. Thompson, I need your signature on this contract.

Mr. Thompson:
Ethan, can you tell I'm on the telephone?

Ethan:
It will take just a second.

Role Play

Mr. Thompson:
Ethan, it can wait.

Ethan:
Well, Okay.

Teacher's Guide

Using Formal Language

Purpose:

To provide the students with examples of the effect of standard versus slang English.

Objectives:

The students will:

1. Approximate standard English usage for interviews.
2. See how slang sounds in an interview context.

Procedures:

1. Ask the students to list the things that an employer would look for when they are first talking with a prospective employee. List some of these on the board.
2. Select the students to participate in the role play.
3. Begin the role play.

For Scene 1, the part of Rochelle is left blank for the student to ad lib using street, slang, or fad language. The topic of what needs to be addressed is provided. For this part you may wish to have a second student assisting the Rochelle part. The second student would assist by suggesting to Rochelle what she might say next.

For Scene 2, proceed as usual.

4. Discuss with the students the effects of slang, street, or fad language on the listener and the importance of using standard English when working in a business so that misunderstandings will be minimized.
5. Complete the worksheet.

Discussion suggestions:

1. When is street, fad, or slang language acceptable?
2. How do dialects and language pathologies differ from street, fad, or slang?

Enrichment:

Use the discussions suggestions

Worksheet:

Using Formal Language

Worksheet

Using Formal Language

Answer true or false for the following statements:

_____ Formal language is better understood by more people than slang, fad, or street language.

_____ Employers will be favorably impressed if you use slang.

_____ Your search for work will be more successful if you use formal language.

_____ Misunderstandings between people happen more often by using formal language.

_____ Employers will make some judgments about your ability to do their work by the language you use.

_____ Street, fad, or slang language is NOT bad or wrong when used among your friends.

_____ Most people can use more than one form of language.

Role Play

Using Formal Language
Scene 1:

Rochelle, a high school student, is asking a business owner if she has any job openings. Rochelle is using street, slang, or fad language.
They are in the office of the business.

Rochelle:
What's up?

Ms. Chapman:
May I help you?

Rochelle:
I heard you needed some help.

Ms. Chapman:
I may be needing someone to assist in the front office.

Rochelle:
Like, what would I do?

Ms. Chapman:
For one thing you would be required to wait on customers at the counter.

Rochelle:
Way cool! I can do it!

Ms. Chapman:
At times you would be asked to deliver things to some of our customers, get receipts signed, and collect some checks.

Role Play

Ms. Chapman is showing some lack of interest.

Rochelle:
Wow, like all that is just for me! What else would I do?

Ms. Chapman appears to be uninterested.

Ms. Chapman:
That will be all. If you like, you may leave your application with the secretary.

Ms. Chapman leaves the room quickly.

Scene 2:
Same as Scene 1, except that Rochelle is using standard formal business English.

Rochelle:
Hello, my name is Rochelle. I am looking for part-time employment.

Ms. Chapman:
Yes, I may be needing someone to assist in the front office.

Rochelle:
That would be interesting. What would the duties include?

Ms. Chapman:
For one thing you would be required to wait on customers at the counter.

Rochelle:
Oh, great! I enjoy meeting with helping people. I would enjoy that.
Are there other duties?

Ms. Chapman:

Yes, at times you would be asked to deliver things to some of our customers, get receipts signed, and collect some checks.

Ms. Chapman is smiling.

Rochelle:

How nice! A chance to get out a little, too. I've had training for handling checks, preparing receipts, and using good communications.
I could handle those duties.

Ms. Chapman asks Rochelle to be seated.

Ms. Chapman:

I'm sure you could. You will need to answer the telephones sometimes and take messages.

Rochelle:

The job would provide a lot of experience. In my vocational training classes we have learned to answer telephones and to make sure the messages are correct.
May I apply.

Ms. Chapman:

I don't think that will be necessary, Rochelle. When can you begin work?

Teacher's Guide

Clarifying Instructions

Purpose:
To get across the idea that it is better to ask and be correct than to not ask and be incorrect.

Objectives:
The students will:

1. Ask for directions to be repeated for better understanding.
2. Write directions that are long or complex.

Procedures:

1. Pose a question to your students. How would an employer view an employee that asks for instructions to be repeated? Let the students debate the questions for a few minutes.
2. Select students to participate in the role play.
3. Begin the role play.

For Scene 1, the student players will be unsuccessful because they fail to get a clarification of their instructions. At the conclusion of Scene 1, ask the students what Robert and Laura needed to do to be more successful?

For Scene 2, ask the students to compare the results. You may ask if any of the students have had similar experiences.

4. Discuss the need to clarify instructions and directions. This is particularly important when there are some words that are not understood or are not familiar to the worker.
5. Complete the worksheet.

Discussions suggestions:

1. When does a worker look best? When they ask and get it right? Or, when they don't ask and get it wrong?
2. How can you ask for clarifications when the people you are working with don't want to ask?

Enrichment:
Ask the principal to visit the class and discuss with the students her/his experiences of supervising people and trying to get instructions understood.

Worksheet:
Clarifying Instructions

Worksheet

Clarifying Instructions

Place a check mark in front of the statements with which you agree.

_____ Work bosses like to repeat instructions more than they like to have work done wrong.

_____ I look smarter asking for instructions to be repeated than I do getting the work done wrong.

_____ Getting the work done wrong could get me fired from my job.

_____ Looking smart is hard if you do the job wrong.

_____ The time to begin getting the job right is by getting the instructions right.

_____ Writing instructions to use as a guide is good, particularly if the instructions are complicated.

_____ A good worker is a correct worker.

_____ Getting a job right the first time is quicker than doing it twice.

Role Play

Clarifying Instructions
Scene 1:

*Robert and Laura are working. Their boss, Ms. Taylor,
has instructed them on what they need to do.*

Robert:
Laura, how did Ms. Taylor say to complete this inventory?

Laura:
She said to just list the products by number and then count them.

Robert:
I thought she said to list them by name, then use the numbers, and then count.

Laura:
Whatever she said, we were supposed to use this form to list the products before we count them.

Robert:
No, we were supposed to count them first.

Laura:
Here comes Ms. Taylor. We'd better ask.

Robert:
If we ask her we will look really dumb. All that matters is that we get it all done.

Laura:
But, what if we get it done and it's wrong?

Role Play

Robert:
We can figure it out. Come on. Let's get moving so she won't think something is wrong.

Four hours later.

Laura:
Robert, I've finished this section.

Robert:
Good, I'll be finished soon and we can put the inventory together.

Laura:
It looks pretty good.

Robert:
Here she comes. Let's turn it in to her and see what she thinks.

Ms. Taylor:
Oh, how nice that you're finished.

Laura:
We worked really hard.

Ms. Taylor:
I'm sure you did. But where are the categories, and the complete accounting sheets, and the …

Robert:
I think - I think we didn't think.

Role Play

Scene 2:
A similar setting to Scene 1, but with a different outcome.

Robert:

Laura, how did Ms. Taylor say to complete this inventory?

Laura:

She said to just list the products by number and then count them.

Robert:

I thought she said to list them by name, then use the numbers,
and then list the count.

Laura:

Whatever she said, we were supposed to use this form to list the products
before we counted them.

Robert:

No, we were supposed to count them first.

Laura:

Here comes Ms. Taylor. We had better ask.

Robert:

Right. It will be better to ask now than to be wrong later.

Laura:

Ms. Taylor, we need some help remembering your instructions.

Ms. Taylor:

Sure. It's better to get it right the first time.

Robert:

We have the instructions all confused.

Ms. Taylor:

It can be confusing. Let's write down a guide for you to follow.

Laura:

I'll write it down as you repeat the instructions.

Ms. Taylor:

I need to write things down often. I never think it is bad for others to make sure they have instructions just right.

Robert:

You mean it doesn't make us look dumb to take more time to ask questions or write down instructions?

Ms. Taylor:

Wouldn't it take a lot longer if you did the whole job wrong?

Laura:

I don't even want to think about it.

Ms. Taylor:

Neither do I. I really prefer for employees to be responsible enough to make sure they understand instructions. Now, are you ready?

Teacher's Guide

Using Electronic Communications

Purpose:

To provide general guidelines regarding the use of telephones, E-mail, and FAXs in the workplace.

Objectives:

The students will:

1. Demonstrate appropriate business telephone manners (who, what, where).
2. Describe theft to include inappropriate work and equipment time for personal use.
3. Students will demonstrate when they should ask for assistance using electronic equipment.

Procedures:

1. With the students in total group, ask for a volunteer to demonstrate how they would make a business call to a customer that had called earlier. Let the individual demonstrate. Then, ask the class for constructive ideas.
2. Select students for the role play. Up to seven students may participate.
3. Conduct the role play.
4. Discuss after each scene, using the following as a guide:

Scene 1. Ask the class if they think that it was right that Jake got fired? How was Jake stealing? What does the term 'unauthorized use' mean?

Scene 2. Ask the students if they noticed the Who, What and Why aspects of Mona's telephone call? Is that a good procedure for business calls?

Scene 3. Is it better to ask and get it correct, don't ask and make a mistake, or break the equipment? 'Ask First' is the rule.

5. Complete the worksheet: Using Electronic Equipment.

Discussion suggestions:

1. What is theft?
2. Can you steal time?

Enrichment:

Ask a local member of the Chamber of Commerce if they would come to class and discuss the issue with the students.

Worksheet:

Using Electronic Communications

Worksheet

Using Electronic Communications
Place a check mark in front of your choices.

It is possible to misuse which of the following items:

_____ time   _____ paper

_____ equipment   _____ tools

_____ telephone   _____ computers

_____ FAX machines

Complete the statements below by using what, why, who.

Good telephone manners for business includes telling the people you call:

_____ you are.

_____ you are calling.

_____ you want.

Complete the following statement:

When you are unsure of how to use a piece of equipment you should:

Ask _____ !

Role Play

Using Electronic Communications
Scene 1:
Jake talking with his girl friend, Peg.

Jake:
Sure, I'll send you a FAX of the whole party thing.

Peg:
That will be great, I didn't know you had a FAX.

Jake:
I don't. I'm at work now and I'll send it from here.

Peg:
Are you sure that will be all right?

Jake:
Hey, it's no big deal just a few copies and a FAX.

Peg:
Sure, it just a few copies, and a FAX, and this long distance call.

Jake:
Everyone does it. It is like a fringe benefit of working here.

Peg:
I'll look forward to getting all of the stuff.

A few days later, Peg calling Jake.

Role Play

Peg:

Hi, Jake, its me.

Jake:

I'm glad you called.

Peg:

Weren't you going to send the stuff for me?

Jake:

Well I was but I couldn't. I got fired. They said I was stealing when I was making personal calls, copies, and FAXing stuff.

Peg:

That's really a hard place to work.

Jake:

They said that I should use my time at work for business only. They also said that the use of equipment for personal use was inappropriate.

Scene 2:
Using the telephone correctly and with manners

Mona:

Hello, this is Mona, from Central Supplies. I'm returning a call to Mr. Customer.

Mr. Customer:

Yes, Mona, this is Mr. Customer. What I need is . . .

Role Play

Mona:

I understand perfectly, Mr. Customer, but I am not as knowledgeable about that as Ms. Boss. If you don't mind I would like to transfer your call to her.

Mr. Customer:

That seems like it would be best, thank you.

Ms. Boss:

Mr. Customer, this is Ms. Boss, I understand that you need information regarding . . .

Scene 3:
Kevin is being asked to do something.

Mr. Chance:

Kevin, would you go make 10 copies of each of these, please.

Kevin:

Sure, Mr. Chance. You wanted 10 each, correct?

Mr. Chance:

That is correct. Thank you Kevin.

Kevin: *(To himself)*

I'll just try and figure out how to make these copies. If I just do this. No, that didn't work. Well, I could . . .

Ms. Wonder: *(she just happens to be walking by)* Do you need help, Kevin?

Role Play

Kevin:

Well, I ugh, yes, I do, Ms. Wonder.

Ms. Wonder:

You just watch me and then you try, OK?

Kevin:

I think I can do that.

Ms. Wonder:

That's right, Kevin.

Kevin:

It was easy!

Ms. Wonder:

It is if you do it correctly. If you don't, the machine may jam and then it's out of service while someone fixes it.

Kevin:

Is it hard to fix?

Ms. Wonder:

Not usually, but it probably won't happen if when you need help and don't know how to do it you ask first.

Kevin:

Oh, what a great idea, ask first!

Teacher's Guide

Business Talk Only

Purpose:
To teach students to talk about business only while in the work place and keep personal information and gossip out of the job site

Objectives:
The students will:

1. Describe the type of conversations that are acceptable in the work place.

2. Demonstrate what they can do when an inappropriate conversation occurs near them.

3. Demonstrate helpful, not hurtful, interpersonal interactions.

Procedures:

1. With the students in total group ask them to list interactions that are inappropriate during math lessons. List a few of these on the board and ask the students how the appropriate conversation during math is similar to appropriate conversations in the work place.
   Key points: They need to be about the topic, the questions should be for clarification, and they need to be helpful with no distracting comments.

2. Select students for the role play. Eight students may participate.

3. Conduct the role play one scene at a time with discussions after each scene.

Essential points of each scene:

Scene 1. Inappropriate talk except for Carl. What did Carl do?

Scene 2. Inappropriate personal problems. What did Tom do? He tried to return the conversation to business and finally left to do what he knew he needed to do.
What happened with Nila?

Scene 3. Appropriate business talk.

Teacher's Guide

Discussion suggestions:

Scene 1. Why should rumors not be repeated?

What can you do when you are hearing rumors?

Scene 2. Why do personal problems not belong in the work place?

What can you do if someone tries to tell you their personal

Scene 3. What is included in appropriate business talk?

Enrichment:

Invite a local company's personnel director to talk to the class.

Complete the worksheet:

Business Talk Only

Worksheet

Business Talk Only

Place YES in front of the statements that are appropriate for work.

_____ Your car broke.

_____ You need help with a task at work.

_____ You are broke.

_____ Your girlfriend/boyfriend is mad at you.

_____ You are not sure what to do and you ask about it.

_____ You heard from a friend that the job hours were going to change.

_____ You have a headache and you tell your coworkers.

_____ You need to ask if you can leave your work station.

_____ You don't like the boss and you are going to tell her so.

Role Play

Business Talk Only
Scene 1:
Workers on break at work.

Jeb:
Did you hear that our company is going to be bought out?

Jan:
Sure, and I heard that the boss is going to get rich and all of us will be out of work.

Carl:
Sounds like bad rumors to me.

Jeb:
I think it's the truth

Carl:
Jeb, don't go spreading rumors that you don't know anything about.

Jan:
Well, everyone knows that the boss is not going to look out for us.

Carl:
I don't know that, and I am not going to be part of this conversation.

Carl leaves the scene.

Jan:
I've heard that the boss hires him to do work outside of here.

Role Play

Jeb:

No wonder he sticks up for him. Maybe we can't trust him!

Note: Discuss Scene 1 at this point. See Teacher's Guide.

Scene 2:
Workers talking while working on a project.

Tom:

How are you doing today, Nila?

Nila:

Not too well, Tom.

Tom:

I'm sorry to hear that, Nila.

Nila:

Well, thank you but you know that I had a car accident.

Tom:

No, I didn't. I hope everything is OK.

Nila:

Well, it isn't. The insurance company is not agreeing with what I think they owe me.

Tom:

That is the way things go.

Role Play

Nila:

Well, I may need to sue them if they don't come around.

Tom:

I need to get this stuff over to the office.

Nila:

I can see you aren't interested.

Tom:

I need to get my work done, Nila.

Nila:

You can get it done, but …

Tom:

Really, I need to go.

Tom leaves the area.

Mr. Albert:

Nila, do you have that material I asked you to get?

Nila:

Right away, Mr. Albert.

Mr. Albert:

Get the material and then we need to talk about your job performance.

Note: Discuss Scene 2 at this point. See Teacher's Guide.

Role Play

Scene 3:

Workers using good business talk.

Joe:
How are you doing, Tom?

Tom:
Nothing to complain about, Joe.

Joe:
Can you give me a hand lifting this?

Tom:
Sure, be glad too.

Marie:
Hi, guys. Can you two go over to the office when you are finished with that?

Joe:
Sure, Marie, be glad to go.

Tom:
Marie, were you able to get more instructions on what we need to do in the warehouse?

Marie:
Sure. I'll let you know when you come over to the office.

Tom:
Thanks, Marie. Be there shortly.

Role Play

Joe:

She sure is a lot of help when I have questions about something.

Tom:

It's a pleasure to work with her.

Note: Discuss Scene 3 at this point. See Teacher's Guide.

Chapter Ten

Social Communications

Teacher's Guide

Social Introductions

Purpose:
To familiarize students with socially appropriate protocol for making introductions.

Objectives:
The students will:
1. Demonstrate how to introduce themselves to individuals they have not previously met.
2. Demonstrate how to introduce individuals who have not met each other.
3. Demonstrate appropriate protocol for introductions.
4. Use the other person's name when acknowledging the introductions.

Procedures:
1. Ask students if they have ever been uncomfortable in groups where introductions were not made. Let them discuss their feelings.
2. Select individuals to participate in the role play.
3. Conduct the role plays.
4. Allow time for follow-up questions and discussions. Point out to the students the protocol of when first names, last names, and titles are used.
5. Complete the worksheet.

Discussions suggestions:
1. How would cultural differences affect introductions?
2. How do differing ages affect introductions?
3. How can introductions affect the way individuals feel in a group?

Enrichment:
1. Ask the students when they watch TV to observe how people are introduced in movies, on talk shows, on the news, etc. Follow up at a prescribed time with discussions of what they have observed.

Worksheet:
Social Introductions

Worksheet

Social Introductions

Put a check mark in front of each rule of introductions that was presented in the role play. Write a plus sign in front of rules that were not in the role play but are good introduction rules.

_____ Generally, the person who knows the other people should initiate the introductions.

_____ Use Mr., Mrs., or Ms. when introduced to adults until they let you know that first names are appropriate.

_____ When first meeting someone you have never met you should greet them by telling them your name.

_____ In a group, if no one else initiates the introductions, you should do so.

_____ When you are introduced to a person it is helpful to repeat their name by saying, "It's nice to meet you, John."

Role Play

Social Introductions
Scene:

Lindsey is getting ready to go help her new neighbor clean her yard. Her father, John Stewart, is going to the neighbor's house a little later than her because neither of them have personally met the neighbor.

John Stewart:
What time are you going to the neighbor's house?

Lindsey:
She asked that I be there at noon.

John Stewart:
What is her name?

Lindsey:
Mrs. Sara McLaughlin. Are you coming over, Dad?

John Stewart:
Yes. I would like to meet our new neighbor.

Lindsey:
I'll see you over there. I'm leaving now.

John leaves the scene and Lindsey arrives at Mrs. McLaughlin's house. Lindsey rings the doorbell and Mrs. McLaughlin answers the door.

Lindsey:
Hello, Mrs. McLaughlin. I am Lindsey Stewart, and it's nice to finally meet you in person.

Role Play

Mrs. McLaughlin:

It is so nice to meet you, Lindsey, and it very nice of you to assist me.

Lindsey:

I'm pleased that you ask me to help. By the way, my father will stop by shortly to meet you.

Mrs. McLaughlin:

That will be nice. I'm anxious to meet my new neighbors.

John Stewart steps back into the scene.

Lindsey:

Mrs. McLaughlin, this my father, John Stewart. Dad, this is Mrs. McLaughlin.

John Stewart:

It's nice to meet you, Mrs. McLaughlin, and to welcome you to the neighborhood.

Mrs. McLaughlin:

It's very nice to meet Lindsey's father, Mr. Stewart. And please call me Sara.

John Stewart:

Very well, Sara, but, only if you will call me John. I think I had better get out of the way of this work.

Mrs. McLaughlin:

Thank you for stopping by, John. It is a pleasure to have met you.

John Stewart leaves the scene and Sarah, a friend of Lindsey's, is walking by.

Role Play

Lindsey:
Mrs. McLaughlin, do you want these leaves raked?

Mrs. McLaughlin:
Yes, Lindsey, and then we will cut those weeds.

Lindsey:
Hi, Sarah. I haven't seen you for a while.

Sarah:
Hi, Lindsay. It has been a while, but I thought you lived over there.

Lindsey:
I do, but I'm helping Mrs. McLaughlin with some yard work.

Sarah:
That's neighborly of you.

Lindsey:
Sarah, I would like you to meet our new neighbor, Mrs. McLaughlin.
Mrs. McLaughlin, this is my friend Sarah.

Sarah:
It's nice to meet you Mrs. McLaughlin.

Mrs. McLaughlin:
It is nice to meet you, too, Sarah.

Sarah:
I need to go or I'll be late. Mrs. McLaughlin, I hope you like the neighborhood.

Role Play

Mrs. McLaughlin:
I'm sure I will, thank you.

Lindsey:
Bye, Sarah. See you at school.

Sarah:
Bye.

Teacher's Guide

Dealing with Angry People

Purpose:
To provide students with an effective method of dealing with people who are angry.

Objectives:
The students will:

1. Use a prescribed effective formula for dealing with people who are angry.
2. Be able to recite the formula for dealing with angry people.

Procedures:

1. Ask the students what they do when dealing with a person who is angry. Record some of the responses on the board. Inquire if they are satisfied with the results?
2. Select students to participate in the role play.
3. Begin the role play.
4. Review with the students the essential principles: The best rule is don't deal with people when they (or you) are angry. But, for the purpose of this role play it is assumed that the interaction must take place.

For Scene 1:
   - What needs to be done.
   - Acknowledge the person's feelings.
   - Restate their statements of what caused the anger
   - Ask for an action(s) that would resolve the issue.
   - Negotiate, if needed.

For Scene 2:
   - Mistakes often made.
   - Telling the other person to be calm doesn't work.
   - Defending your or other's actions doesn't work.
   - Giving advice is rarely well received.

5. Discuss the need to develop a personal style after learning the role play procedures.
6. Complete the worksheet.

Teacher's Guide

Discussion suggestions:

1. Why doesn't giving advice generally work?
2. What happens if you try to defend your actions that allegedly caused the anger?

Enrichment:

Ask the students how the procedure would work with their boss on a job?

Worksheet:

Dealing with Angry People

Worksheet

Dealing with Angry People

The guide words for dealing with people who are angry are:

A _____

R _____

A _____

N _____

When possible, the best method of dealing with angry people

is to wait until they are _____.

As a general rule some things that do not work for dealing with people who are angry are:

Tell them to be c _____.

D_____ yourself or others.

Give _____.

Role Play

Dealing with Angry People
Scene 1:
Aaron and Sally are walking home from school.
Aaron is telling of his encounter with Mike.

Aaron:

Wow, Mike was really mad today!

Rhonda:

What was his problem?

Aaron:

He had had a run in with Mr. Teacher and it did not go well.

Rhonda:

And Mike ended up angry?

Aaron:

Yes, he was really in a rage.

Rhonda:

What did you do?

Aaron:

I tried to use the stuff we were taught in the Life Studies class. You know, avoid dealing with angry people if possible, then acknowledge, restate, ask, and negotiate. Of course, I didn't need to negotiate because he wasn't mad at me, he was angry with Mr. Teacher.

Rhonda:

Well, how did it work?

Role Play

Aaron:

Really well. I couldn't avoid him, or deal with him later, so I just acknowledged that he was pretty steamed by saying 'He really got you angry didn't he?' and he immediately agreed with that.

Rhonda:

And then, did he start to talk about it?

Aaron:

Did he ever! And as he talked I just restated the main points of what he said. Like he would say that Mr. Teacher should not deal with things that are between two students if it doesn't affect class. Then I would say, 'So he should mind his own business.'

Rhonda:

Could you see him calming down as you went through this restating step?

Aaron:

Yes, it was really obvious. Then, as he got calmer I asked him what he thought could be done now? You know that 'Ask for a solution' part of the plan we learned.

Rhonda:

I know Mike pretty well. I imagine he had some ideas.

Aaron:

He sure did. We discussed a few and he decided to go see Mr. Teacher tomorrow and apologize for his anger, and then ask him how they could avoid such scenes in the future.

Rhonda:

I hope he remembers to approach him in private and not in front of a lot of students.

Aaron:

He said he will go to his office. Once they get a few ideas out in the open they will be able to negotiate on a good decision for the two of them.

Rhonda:

That really worked. Acknowledge. Restate. Ask. Negotiate.

Scene 2:
*Mike and Sara are talking. Mike is very angry at Mr. Teacher.
It is not going well for them.*

Mike:

And, then Mr. Teacher said that I was not making good choices.

Sara:

Mike, you just need to calm down. It is not that big a deal.

Mike:

To you it's not a big deal. I think he stepped way over the line.

Sara:

Let it go, Mike, you can't win anyway.

Mike:

We'll see about that.

Role Play

Sara:

He was just trying to do what he thought was right.

Mike:

It's hard to believe that my best friend is against me, too.

Sara:

I'm not against you. But you need to calm down and recognize that you can't win against a teacher.

Mike:

How would you like it if he did that to you? I suppose you would just let it go, right?

Sara:

It's not about me. If I were you I would calm down and try to get on his good side.

Mike:

And you used to be my friend.

Teacher's Guide

Whoops, My Error

Purpose:

To assist students in learning how to acknowledge when they have made an error.

Objectives:

The students will:

1. Demonstrate socially appropriate acceptance of mistakes.
2. Demonstrate how to take corrective action for their errors.

Procedures:

1. With the students in a class group, ask how many of them have made mistakes? Then, ask for volunteers to describe what they did after the mistake. If all of the examples are models of good practice, ask if any of the students have seen someone try to cover up their mistakes.
2. Select students to participate in the role play.
3. Conduct the role play.
4. Review with the students the essential steps:
   • Acknowledge
   • Correct or move on
   • Find a better way
5. Ask students where they might try this approach to correcting errors.
6. Complete the worksheet.

Discussion suggestions:

1. Why do some people have so much difficulty admitting they made a mistake?
2. What happens when you try to hide a mistake instead of correcting it?

Enrichment:

Assign the students to watch for examples of appropriate and inappropriate ways that people handle their mistakes at school or out in the community.

Worksheet:

Whoops, My Error

Worksheet

Whoops, My Error

Circle the answer or answers that are correct for each statement.
You may circle more than one answer for each statement.

1. Admitting a mistake is good because it:
   • gets things corrected quickly
   • avoids blaming others
   • allows you to learn better ways to do things
   • may keep other mistakes from happening

2. When you blame others for your errors:
   • they may get mad
   • they will like the blame and ask you for more

3. If you can correct the mistake you will first need to:
   • blame others
   • admit the mistake was made

4. What is important is that:
   • others get the blame
   • mistakes get corrected
   • you learn how to do things better.

Acknowledge
Correct
Find a better way

Role Play

Whoops, My Error
Scene 1:
Students are talking about missing a club meeting.

Joan:

I missed the meeting, but Shane didn't send out a second notice about the meeting.

Pete:

He did put the information in the school paper.

Joan:

Well, that wasn't enough.

Pete:

It's a big thing that you just missed the meeting.

Joan:

I was going to run for vice president and now Sherry is vice president.

Jack:

I feel awful that you wanted to run for office and missed the meeting.

Joan:

I wouldn't have missed it if Shane had sent a second notice.

Pete:

But why is it Shane's problem that you missed the meeting?

Role Play

Joan:

I told you, already!

Jack:

Everyone else was at the meeting and they didn't get a second meeting notice.

Joan:

I can see that you two are no help. You just think that it is right that Sherry is vice president instead of me.

Pete:

Joan, please don't take it out on us. We're your friends.

Joan:

Some friends. You're against me!

Scene 2:
Pete and Jack are talking with Ms. Ray.

Pete:

Joan really is steamed about the meeting.

Jack:

Right, but she should accept her own mistake.

Ms. Ray:

It is often difficult to accept that you have made a mistake.

Role Play

Pete:

Especially, when she missed out on running for office.

Ms. Ray:

Yes, then it may be even harder.

Jack:

There were some steps to take from Life Problems class.

Ms. Ray:

I'm pleased that you're remembering them, and I wish that Joan would remember, too.

Jack:

The first step is the hardest. It is to just acknowledge the mistake you made.

Pete:

Acknowledge means admit it, doesn't it?

Ms. Ray:

That's correct. And it can be the most difficult part.

Jack:

It seems that once you admit your mistake instead of hiding it or blaming someone else, the rest should be easier.

Pete:

Right! The next step is to correct the error or move on if there is no correction to be made.

Role Play

Ms. Ray:

How could Joan correct the error?

Jack:

She can't now, but it's over and she should move ahead with other things.

Pete:

She can correct how she keeps track of events that she's interested in attending or doing.

Ms. Ray:

That sounds like a good idea. How would she do that?

Jack:

She could write things down when she first knows about them.

Pete:

That would keep her from making the same mistake again.

Jack:

And, then, she would not need to be mad at us.

Ms. Ray:

Sounds like everyone would be better off. So what are the steps she or you can take?

Pete:

First, when you recognize a mistake you need to admit it and accept it.

Role Play

Jack:

Then you need to correct it if you can.

Pete:

Finally, you need to find a better way to do things so you won't make the same mistake again.

Ms. Ray:

Good, you have all three steps!

Jack:

Look, there is Joan now. Should we remind her of the steps?

Pete:

Maybe tomorrow when she is calmer.

Teacher's Guide

It Is Not What You Say

Purpose:
To have students become familiar with some of the nonverbal cues that are used to determine sincerity and honesty.

Objectives:
The students will:

1. Identify four aspects of nonverbal language that give others information about you.
2. Identify two negative aspects of using inappropriate nonverbal language.

Procedures:

1. Group students in small groups and ask them to list ways we send messages to others without using spoken or written language. List their ideas on the board and save for discussion after the role play.
2. Select three students to participate in the role play.
3. Conduct the role play.
4. Review with the students the essential aspects of nonverbal behavior:
    - eye contact
    - posture
    - tone
    - inflection

    Compare these essential aspects with what the students listed in the introductory activity.
5. Complete the worksheet: It Is Not What You Say

Discussions suggestions:

1. What are other aspects of nonverbal language?
2. Would nonverbal language be important on the telephone?

Enrichment:
Ask students to watch a television show and report the nonverbal language they saw and how it affected the meaning of what people were saying verbally.

Worksheet:
It Is Not What You Say

Worksheet

It Is Not What You Say

Complete the sentences using the words at the bottom of the page.

When I am talking with another person I need to maintain _____ contact,

stand or sit with good _____ , use an appropriate _____ ,

and be careful how I say something, it is called _____ .

Tone

Posture

Inflection

Eye

Role Play

It Is Not What You Say
Scene:
Three students having a discussion.

Jill:
I have trouble believing what you say, Mort.

Mort:
Why would you not believe what I'm telling you?

Jill:
I'm t sure. But when you tell me why you did that it just doesn't feel right.

Mort:
It doesn't feel right?

Jim:
Same for me, Mort, it's just that - it's just that you're hard to believe.

Mort:
Sure is great to be among friends.

Jill:
You said Mr. Salas wasn't sure that you were telling it like it really was, either.

Mort:
Right! First him, now both of you! Why don't you believe me?

Role Play

Jim:

One of things that bothers me is that you look away when you tell me about it, instead of looking at me.

Mort:

Like that's a big deal.

Jill:

It seems that most people look at you when they talk. It seems to help make a connection with the other person.

Jim:

Looking at the person would help a lot.

Mort:

Okay, so you don't like that I don't look at you. But is that enough to not believe me?

Jill:

Well, if you really want to know, Mort, you also get loud when you begin to tell the details of what happened.

Mort:

That's the way I am, that's all.

Jim:

Hey, Mort, you asked us, remember?

Jill:

It may be the way you are and you may tell the truth, but if no one believes . . .

Role Play

Mort:
So I need to look at you and not get louder when someone asks for details?

Jim:
Right.

Mort:
Then you'll believe me?

Jill:
Well, it will help.

Jim:
You remember that kid that came here for only a couple of months? The one no one would believe anything he said?

Mort:
I remember, but I'm not like him!

Jill:
No, but there are some things you do like he did.

Jim:
He didn't look at people and he would get loud when asked to support his ideas.

Jill:
He would start moving around and act nervous if someone asked him questions.

Mort:

So what should I do? I'm telling the truth.

Jim:

Remember in Life Skills class we talked about 'nonverbal behavior?'

Mort:

Sure, I remember. The way you act tells people a lot about your interest, attitude . . . and maybe if your telling the truth?

Jill:

That's the way I remember it. You need to look at people when you speak.

Mort:

And when they speak!

Jim:

Right! You need to keep your tone appropriate for the situations.

Jill:

Don't forget to sound like you mean what you say so you don't send the wrong message.

Mort:

For example, I can say something like 'That's great" and mean several different things just by the way I say it?

Jim:

Yes, the tone of your voice says a lot and can send a meaning that you didn't intend to send. That is called inflection.

Role Play

Jill:
There sure is a lot more to talking than just words.

Jim:
I remember from class that your posture is important, too!

Mort:
Thanks, I think I've got some good ideas.

Teacher's Guide

Listening Actively

Purpose:

For students to learn how to provide their partners in conversation with feedback that lets them know they are listening to them and being attentive.

Objectives:

The students will:

1. Demonstrate the ability to consider and encourage the other person's ideas.
2. Demonstrate following up on the other person's statements
3. Demonstrate the ability to wait to interject their thoughts.

Procedures:

1. Make two list headings on the chalkboard. One titled 'Feel Good' and the other titled 'Not so Good.' Then ask the students to provide examples that make them feel good or not so good. List the ideas. Save them for a discussion later.
2. Select players for the role play. There can be six different players.
3. Conduct the role play.

Students may benefit from some discussion after each scene of the role play. The essential ideas of the scenes are:

Scene 1. Communication is difficult when neither person hears and/or responds to the other's needs or interests. Conflicts may occur.

Scene 2. A person feels better when listened to by another person. It shows the listener cares about the needs of the speaker and is concerned.

Scene 3. The students discuss the three points listed below and how it feels to have someone listen to them.

4. Discuss the major components of listening actively. Let the other person express their point. To let the other person know you are interested, follow up on their topic. Change topic only when they are finished.
5. Complete the worksheet.

Discussion suggestion:

1. Is it possible to say nothing and yet 'listen actively?'

Worksheet:

Listening Actively

Worksheet

Listening Actively

Place a check in front of the statements that indicate that good skills were being used by the all of the people in the conversation.

_____ 1. I get frustrated trying to get a word into the conversation.

_____ 2. When I said something I know the others were listening because they responded to what I said.

_____ 3. It often felt like two or three conversations were going on at once.

_____ 4. When it was over I felt good.

_____ 5. An hour after I tried to tell the group about the event two of the people asked me the exact thing that I had tried to tell them.

_____ 6. One of the people always switched the topic to her interests.

_____ 7. I felt I heard when one person would summarize what I had tried to explain.

_____ 8. No one got upset and everyone seemed to understand what needed to happen next.

Role Play

Listening Actively
Scene 1:
Two students walking across campus.

Tyler:
I need to go to see Mr. Gee about that test I took.

Sybil:
Yeah, I need to go get some new gym shoes after school.

Tyler:
I'm really worried about the test. I didn't do well.

Sybil:
Which color shoes should I get, Tyler?

Tyler:
Frankly, Sybil, I couldn't care less!

Sybil:
Get a life, Tyler!

Scene 2:
Two different students having a discussion.

Ray:
I'm really concerned about my Life Skills class.

Sis:
What about it concerns you, Ray?

Role Play

Ray:

I'll miss next week because of the field trip and some appointments.

Sis:

So you're afraid you'll get behind in the assignments?

Ray:

That's right, Sis. And, will I be able to catch up?

Sis:

What are you doing to make arrangements for being gone?

Ray:

I've got an appointment to see Mr. Gee after school today.

Sis:

Well, it seems like you and he will be able to come to a solution.

Ray:

I think so. I'm probably worried before I need to be.

Sis:

Let me know what I can do.

Ray:

Thanks for listening, Sis. Weren't you going shopping after school?

Sis:

Yes. I am so excited!

Role Play

Scene 3:

Ray talking with two other students about talking.

Sue:

Have you ever noticed that there are some people you like to talk with more than others.

Ray:

Sure! I like to talk with Sis.

Will:

Why is that, Ray?

Ray:

She makes me feel like she is interested in what I am saying.

Sue:

That would be great. Some people just seem to want to say what they have on their minds.

Will:

It is a helpful skill to be able to listen to what others say.

Ray:

It sure helps if you have some problem that you need to talk about.

Sue:

Remember in Life Skills class how we studied 'active listening?'

Role Play

Will:

Yes, but it's kind of foggy to me.

Ray:

I remember that you should let the other person hear what you heard them say.

Will:

That's right. You do that by following up on what they said.

Sue:

Yes, instead of carrying on with what interests you.

Ray:

Yes, you kind of finish a topic, then you can change it to your interest.

Will:

That would be great. It seems that I never get finished with what I am saying.

Ray:

I think that is what Sis does. She lets you finish before she says her thing.

Sue:

It's no wonder you like to talk with her. I hope you let her get in what she wants to say, too.

Will:

Yeah, it would be easy to never let a good listener say what they want to talk about.

Role Play

Ray:

I guess if both people are good listeners then both people will get to say what they need to say.

Sue:

Is that the way it works when you talk with, Sis?

Ray:

I hope so. I will have to make sure that it does by being a good listener.